Devon & Cornwall

Edited by Jenni Bannister

First published in Great Britain in 2015 by:

Remus House
Coltsfoot Drive
Peterborough
PE2 9BF
Telephone: 01733 890066
Website: www.youngwriters.co.uk

All Rights Reserved
Book Design by Spencer Hart
© Copyright Contributors 2015
SB ISBN 978-1-78443-696-4

Printed and bound in the UK by BookPrintingUK
Website: www.bookprintinguk.com

Foreword

Dear Reader,

Young Writers was established in 1991 with the aim of encouraging writing skills in young people and giving them the opportunity to see their work in print. Poetry is a wonderful way to introduce young children to the idea of rhyme and rhythm and helps learning and development of communication, language and literacy skills.

'My First Poem' was created to introduce nursery and preschool children to this wonderful world of poetry. They were given a template to fill in with their own words, creating a poem that was all about them.

We are proud to present the resulting collection of personal and touching poems in this anthology, which can be treasured for years to come.

Jenni Bannister

Editorial Manager

Contents

Galmpton Preschool, Brixham

Happy Days South West Limited - Treloggan, Newquay

Hartland Preschool, Bideford

Helston Day Nursery, Helston

Pip-Kins Day Nursery, Exeter

Roger's Burrow Nursery, Plymouth

St Teath Preschool, Bodmin

Sara' School Preschool, Exeter

Starcross Playgroup, Exeter

Sticklebricks
Preschool, Barnstaple

The Poems

My First Poem

My name is Anton and I go to preschool,

My best friend is Ashley, who is really cool.

I watch Spider-Man on TV,

Playing football with Daddy is lots of fun for me.

I just love pasta to eat,

And sometimes chocolate for a treat.

Blue is a colour I like a lot,

My gun is the best present I ever got.

My favourite person is William, who is a gem,

So this, my first poem, is just for them!

Anton Locker (3)
Boscastle Playschool, Boscastle

My First Poem

My name is Jak and I go to preschool,

My best friend is Mum, who is really cool.

I watch dinosaurs on TV,

Playing dinosaur games is lots of fun for me.

I just love carrots to eat,

And sometimes chocolate for a treat.

Green is a colour I like a lot,

My stegosaurus is the best present I ever got.

My favourite person is Jade, who is a gem,

So this, my first poem, is just for them!

Jak Bowker (3)
Boscastle Playschool, Boscastle

My First Poem

My name is Sowena and I go to preschool,

My best friend is Phoebe, who is really cool.

I watch Simba and Beauty and the Beast on TV,

Playing hide-and-seek is lots of fun for me.

I just love pasta and cheese to eat,

And sometimes yoghurt for a treat.

Pink is a colour I like a lot,

My castle with the prince and princess is the best present I ever got.

My favourite person is Amber, who is a gem,

So this, my first poem, is just for them!

Sowena Bennett (4)
Boscastle Playschool, Boscastle

3

My First Poem

My name is Summer and I go to preschool,

My best friend is my sister, Sophie, who is really cool.

I watch Tinkerbell on TV,

Playing with Anton is lots of fun for me.

I just love fish and chips to eat,

And sometimes ice cream for a treat.

Bright pink is a colour I like a lot,

My ballerina is the best present I ever got.

My favourite person is Amber, who is a gem,

So this, my first poem, is just for them!

Summer Lowles (4)
Boscastle Playschool, Boscastle

My First Poem

My name is Braelen and I go to preschool,

My best friend is Anton, who is really cool.

I watch Avengers on TV,

Playing turtles and superheroes is lots of fun

for me.

I just love sausages to eat,

And sometimes Love Hearts for a treat.

Blue is a colour I like a lot,

My toy robot is the best present I ever got.

My favourite person is Mummy, who is a gem,

So this, my first poem, is just for them!

Braelen Burnard (3)
Boscastle Playschool, Boscastle

5

My First Poem

My name is Amber and I go to preschool,

My best friend is Mummy, who is really cool.

I watch Let It Go on TV,

Playing with Daddy is lots of fun for me.

I just love spaghetti to eat,

And sometimes apple for a treat.

Pink is a colour I like a lot,

My Elsa pyjamas are the best present I ever got.

My favourite person is Summer, who is a gem,

So this, my first poem, is just for them!

Amber Tucker (3)
Boscastle Playschool, Boscastle

6

My First Poem

My name is Ashley and I go to preschool,

My best friend is Noah, who is really cool.

I watch CBeebies on TV,

Playing Lego Batman is lots of fun for me.

I just love broccoli to eat,

And sometimes chocolate for a treat.

Orange is a colour I like a lot,

My Thomas is the best present I ever got.

My favourite person is Felicity, who is a gem,

So this, my first poem, is just for them!

Ashley Blake (3)
Boscastle Playschool, Boscastle

My First Poem

My name is Jake and I go to preschool,

My best friend is Purdey, who is really cool.

I watch Peppa Pig on TV,

Playing racing cars is lots of fun for me.

I just love roast dinner to eat,

And sometimes chocolate for a treat.

White is a colour I like a lot,

My robot is the best present I ever got.

My favourite person is Amber, who is a gem,

So this, my first poem, is just for them!

Jake Jarvis (3)
Boscastle Playschool, Boscastle

8

My First Poem

My name is Finnley and I go to preschool,

My best friend is Dexter, who is really cool.

I watch Ben 10 on TV,

Playing farms is lots of fun for me.

I just love tuna and jacket potatoes to eat,

And sometimes chocolate for a treat.

Green is a colour I like a lot,

My digger is the best present I ever got.

My favourite person is Mummy, who is a gem,

So this, my first poem, is just for them!

Finnley Dangar (4)
Boscastle Playschool, Boscastle

My First Poem

My name is Flynn and I go to preschool,

My best friend is Ethan, who is really cool.

I watch Ben 10 on TV,

Playing Ben 10 games is lots of fun for me.

I just love pitta, cheese and olives to eat,

And sometimes strawberries for a treat.

Red is a colour I like a lot,

My lion is the best present I ever got.

My favourite person is Mummy, who is a gem,

So this, my first poem, is just for them!

Flynn Roff-Conway (3)
Boscastle Playschool, Boscastle

My First Poem

My name is Archie and I go to preschool,

My best friend is Buddy, who is really cool.

I watch Fireman Sam on TV,

Playing Hungry Hippos is lots of fun for me.

I just love sausages to eat,

And sometimes chocolate and Minion sweets for

a treat.

Black is a colour I like a lot,

My Fireman Sam talking teddy is the best

present I ever got.

My favourite person is Mummy, who is a gem,

So this, my first poem, is just for them!

Archie Herrington (4)
Boscastle Playschool, Boscastle

My First Poem

My name is Purdey and I go to preschool,

My best friend is Amber, who is really cool.

I watch Monster Inc on TV,

Playing hide-and-seek is lots of fun for me.

I just love jacket potato with tuna and

cheese to eat,

And sometimes chocolate for a treat.

Pink is a colour I like a lot,

My robot is the best present I ever got.

My favourite person is Stevie, who is a gem,

So this, my first poem, is just for them!

Purdey Ellis-Atkinson (3)
Boscastle Playschool, Boscastle

My First Poem

My name is Ruben and I go to preschool,

My best friend is Jay, who is really cool.

I watch Ben 10 on TV,

Playing with Nanny is lots of fun for me.

I just love fish fingers and chips to eat,

And sometimes chocolate buttons for a treat.

Dark blue is a colour I like a lot,

My marble game is the best present I ever got.

My favourite person is Sophie, who is a gem,

So this, my first poem, is just for them!

Ruben Johnson (4)
Boscastle Playschool, Boscastle

My First Poem

My name is Sophia and I go to preschool,

My best friend is Ernie, who is really cool.

I watch Tiny Pop on TV,

Playing hide-and-seek is lots of fun for me.

I just love fish and chips to eat,

And sometimes chocolate cake for a treat.

Orange is a colour I like a lot,

My dolly is the best present I ever got.

My favourite person is Mummy, who is a gem,

So this, my first poem, is just for them!

Sophia Anne Clarke (4)
Boscastle Playschool, Boscastle

14

My First Poem

My name is Kiran and I go to preschool,

My best friend is Jaya, who is really cool.

I watch Thomas and Mowgli on TV,

Playing on the beach is lots of fun for me.

I just love fish fingers to eat,

And sometimes sweeties for a treat.

Blue is a colour I like a lot,

My George Pig is the best present I ever got.

My favourite person is Mummy, who is a gem,

So this, my first poem, is just for them!

Kiran Pande (2)
Boscastle Playschool, Boscastle

15

My First Poem

My name is Noah and I go to preschool,

My best friend is Isaac, who is really cool.

I watch Scooby-Doo on TV,

Playing rockets and comics is lots of fun for me.

I just love meat pie to eat,

And sometimes chocolate for a treat.

Orange is a colour I like a lot,

My Ninja Turtle is the best present I ever got.

My favourite person is Mummy, who is a gem,

So this, my first poem, is just for them!

Noah Buxton (4)
Boscastle Playschool, Boscastle

My First Poem

My name is Ernie and I go to preschool,

My best friend is Sophia, who is really cool.

I watch Tree Fu Tom on TV,

Playing jigsaws is lots of fun for me.

I just love carrot soup to eat,

And sometimes chocolate and strawberry ice

cream for a treat.

Purple is a colour I like a lot,

My pirate bedroom is the best present I ever got.

My favourite person is Anton, who is a gem,

So this, my first poem, is just for them!

Ernie Tremain (3)
Boscastle Playschool, Boscastle

17

My First Poem

My name is Jaya and I go to preschool,

My best friend is Kiran, who is really cool.

I watch Peppa Pig on TV,

Playing hide-and-seek is lots of fun for me.

I just love spaghetti to eat,

And sometimes sweet wiggly worms for a treat.

Pink is a colour I like a lot,

My cuddly Ben and Holly toy is the best present I
ever got.

My favourite person is Mummy, who is a gem,

So this, my first poem, is just for them!

Jaya Pande (3)
Boscastle Playschool, Boscastle

My First Poem

My name is Phoebe and I go to preschool,

My best friend is Sowena, who is really cool.

I watch Dora on TV,

Playing roly poly is lots of fun for me.

I just love chicken nuggets to eat,

And sometimes chocolate for a treat.

Pink is a colour I like a lot,

My racing car is the best present I ever got.

My favourite person is Mummy, who is a gem,

So this, my first poem, is just for them!

Phoebe Bennet (3)
Boscastle Playschool, Boscastle

My First Poem

My name is Charlotte and I go to preschool,

My best friend is Rosie, who is really cool.

I watch Peppa Pig on TV,

Playing butterflies is lots of fun for me.

I just love spaghetti and pasta to eat,

And sometimes sweeties for a treat.

Pink is a colour I like a lot,

My bicycle is the best present I ever got.

My favourite person is Sophie, who is a gem,

So this, my first poem, is just for them!

Charlotte Parsons (3)
Boscastle Playschool, Boscastle

My First Poem

My name is Charlotte and I go to preschool,

My best friend is Thomas, who is really cool.

I watch Peppa Pig on TV,

Playing Frozen is lots of fun for me.

I just love sausage and chips to eat,

And sometimes chocolate for a treat.

Pink is a colour I like a lot,

My baby is the best present I ever got.

My favourite person is Mummy, who is a gem,

So this, my first poem, is just for them!

Charlotte Rose Mallows (3)
Caen Caterpillars Preschool, Braunton

My First Poem

My name is Evie and I go to preschool,

My best friend is Georgia, who is really cool.

I watch Peppa Pig on TV,

Playing Mummy and Daddy is lots of fun for me.

I just love carrots to eat,

And sometimes sweeties for a treat.

Red is a colour I like a lot,

My Minnie Mouse jammies are the best present I

ever got.

My favourite person is Mummy, who is a gem,

So this, my first poem, is just for them!

Evie Buckingham (4)
Caen Caterpillars Preschool, Braunton

My First Poem

My name is Bella and I go to preschool,

My best friend is Evie-Rose, who is really cool.

I watch Peppa Pig on TV,

Playing dressing up is lots of fun for me.

I just love Weetabix to eat,

And sometimes cake for a treat.

Red is a colour I like a lot,

My Barbie toy is the best present I ever got.

My favourite person is my dad, who is a gem,

So this, my first poem, is just for them!

Bella Louise Heaton (3)
Caen Caterpillars Preschool, Braunton

My First Poem

My name is Callie and I go to preschool,

My best friend is Mummy, who is really cool.

I watch Peppa Pig on TV,

Playing with dolls is lots of fun for me.

I just love pizza to eat,

And sometimes cake for a treat.

Pink is a colour I like a lot,

My waterfall is the best present I ever got.

My favourite person is Mummy, who is a gem,

So this, my first poem, is just for them!

Callie Scott (2)
Caen Caterpillars Preschool, Braunton

My First Poem

My name is Harvey and I go to preschool,

My best friend is my big brother, Danny, who is really cool.

I watch Toy Story and Wall-E on TV,

Playing with my daddy and my big brother Danny is lots of fun for me.

I just love cheese and crackers and yoghurts to eat,

And sometimes lots of sweeties for a treat.

Green is a colour I like a lot,

My big nut brown hair rabbit is the best present I ever got.

My favourite person is my big Brother Danny, who is a gem,

So this, my first poem, is just for them!

Harvey Wing (3)
Coco's Nursery, Totnes

My First Poem

My name is Ethan and I go to preschool,

My best friend is Jakey D, who is really cool.

I watch Power Rangers on TV,

Playing football is lots of fun for me.

I just love chocolate sandwiches to eat,

And sometimes a biscuit for a treat.

Blue is a colour I like a lot,

My Power Rangers stick is the best present I ever

got.

My favourite person is Mummy, who is a gem,

So this, my first poem, is just for them!

Ethan Green (2)
Coco's Nursery, Totnes

My First Poem

My name is Joseph and I go to preschool,

My best friend is Lilly, who is really cool.

I watch PAW Patrol on TV,

Playing cars is lots of fun for me.

I just love sausages to eat,

And sometimes chocolate for a treat.

Yellow is a colour I like a lot,

My Lightning McQueen is the best present I ever got.

My favourite person is Mumma, who is a gem,

So this, my first poem, is just for them!

Joseph John Barge (2)
Coco's Nursery, Totnes

27

My First Poem

My name is Lily and I go to preschool,

My best friend is Jamie, who is really cool.

I watch SpongeBob SquarePants on TV,

Playing babies is lots of fun for me.

I just love sausage rolls to eat,

And sometimes chocolate for a treat.

Pink is a colour I like a lot,

My princess pencil set is the best present I ever

got.

My favourite person is Poppy, who is a gem,

So this, my first poem, is just for them!

Lily Booker (3)
Coco's Nursery, Totnes

My First Poem

My name is Liam and I go to preschool,

My best friend is William, who is really cool.

I watch Boj on TV,

Playing with my train set is lots of fun for me.

I just love cockles to eat,

And sometimes a Kinder egg for a treat.

Blue is a colour I like a lot,

My blue bike is the best present I ever got.

My favourite person is Mummy, who is a gem,

So this, my first poem, is just for them!

Liam Piper (4)
Coco's Nursery, Totnes

29

My First Poem

My name is Kyle and I go to preschool,

My best friend is Cody, who is really cool.

I watch PAW Patrol on TV,

Playing pirates is lots of fun for me.

I just love breakfast to eat,

And sometimes chocolate for a treat.

Red is a colour I like a lot,

My Spider-Man teddy is the best present I ever got.

My favourite person is Daddy, who is a gem,

So this, my first poem, is just for them!

Kyle Burnard (3)
Delabole Mini Minors Playgroup, Delabole

My First Poem

My name is Cody and I go to preschool,

My best friend is Kyle, who is really cool.

I watch Power Rangers on TV,

Playing swords and pirates is lots of fun for me.

I just love porridge and raisins to eat,

And sometimes sweeties for a treat.

Red is a colour I like a lot,

My big T-rex dinosaur is the best present I ever got.

My favourite person is Somer, who is a gem,

So this, my first poem, is just for them!

Cody Lindsay-Beale (3)
Delabole Mini Minors Playgroup, Delabole

My First Poem

My name is Effie and I go to preschool,

My best friend is Kiera, who is really cool.

I watch Maleficent on TV,

Playing in my kitchen is lots of fun for me.

I just love tuna pasta to eat,

And sometimes chocolate for a treat.

Pink is a colour I like a lot,

My Lamby is the best present I ever got.

My favourite person is Mummy, who is a gem,

So this, my first poem, is just for them!

Effie Worden (3)
Delabole Mini Minors Playgroup, Delabole

My First Poem

My name is Owen and I go to preschool,

My best friend is Cody, who is really cool.

I watch Hulk Smash on TV,

Playing dinosaurs is lots of fun for me.

I just love kiwis to eat,

And sometimes lemonade lollies for a treat.

Orange is a colour I like a lot,

My big boy's bike is the best present I ever got.

My favourite person is Mummy, who is a gem,

So this, my first poem, is just for them!

Owen Dungey (3)
Delabole Mini Minors Playgroup, Delabole

My First Poem

My name is Kiera and I go to preschool,

My best friend is Effie, who is really cool.

I watch Tangled on TV,

Playing Rapunzel is lots of fun for me.

I just love chips to eat,

And sometimes yoghurts for a treat.

Pink is a colour I like a lot,

My bike is the best present I ever got.

My favourite person is Mummy, who is a gem,

So this, my first poem, is just for them!

Kiera Harris (3)
Delabole Mini Minors Playgroup, Delabole

My First Poem

My name is Rosy and I go to preschool,

My best friend is Kyle, who is really cool.

I watch Timmy Time on TV,

Playing with Play-Doh is lots of fun for me.

I just love cheese sandwiches to eat,

And sometimes Christmas ice cream for a treat.

Pink is a colour I like a lot,

My Olaf teddy is the best present I ever got.

My favourite person is Daddy, who is a gem,

So this, my first poem, is just for them!

Rosy Ferguson (2)
Delabole Mini Minors Playgroup, Delabole

My First Poem

My name is Timma and I go to preschool,

My best friend is Keira, who is really cool.

I watch The Little Mermaid on TV,

Playing with Play-Doh is lots of fun for me.

I just love strawberries to eat,

And sometimes an ice lolly for a treat.

Pink is a colour I like a lot,

My Elsa doll is the best present I ever got.

My favourite person is Sam, who is a gem,

So this, my first poem, is just for them!

Tamelia Lewis (2)
Delabole Mini Minors Playgroup, Delabole

My First Poem

My name is William and I go to preschool,

My best friend is Mummy, who is really cool.

I watch CBeebies on TV,

Playing outside is lots of fun for me.

I just love cake to eat,

And sometimes cake for a treat.

Green is a colour I like a lot,

My scooter is the best present I ever got.

My favourite person is Daddy, who is a gem,

So this, my first poem, is just for them!

William Astill (2)

Delabole Mini Minors Playgroup, Delabole

My First Poem

My name is Ronan and I go to preschool,

My best friend is Jake, who is really cool.

I watch farm DVDs on TV,

Playing the computer is lots of fun for me.

I just love cabbage to eat,

And sometimes chocolate sweets for a treat.

Green is a colour I like a lot,

My combine harvester is the best present I ever got.

My favourite person is Karen, who is a gem,

So this, my first poem, is just for them!

Ronan Pearse (3)
Dragonflies, Axminster

My First Poem

My name is Isaiah and I go to preschool,

My best friend is Freddie, who is really cool.

I watch Tractors and Cars on TV,

Playing cars and diggers is lots of fun for me.

I just love toast to eat,

And sometimes fruit for a treat.

Blue is a colour I like a lot,

My digger is the best present I ever got.

My favourite person is Mummy, who is a gem,

So this, my first poem, is just for them!

Isaiah Seth Morris (2)
Dragonflies, Axminster

39

My First Poem

My name is Akshiya and I go to preschool,

My best friend is Roxy, who is really cool.

I watch Peppa Pig on TV,

Playing catch is lots of fun for me.

I just love cheese to eat,

And sometimes strawberries for a treat.

Pink is a colour I like a lot,

My Peppa Pig toy is the best present I ever got.

My favourite person is Daddy, who is a gem,

So this, my first poem, is just for them!

Akshiya Kannan (3)
Dragonflies, Axminster

My First Poem

My name is Freddie and I go to preschool,

My best friend is Isaiah, who is really cool.

I watch Cars on TV,

Playing cars is lots of fun for me.

I just love crisps to eat,

And sometimes a Kinder egg for a treat.

Blue is a colour I like a lot,

My Hot Wheels car is the best present I ever got.

My favourite person is Mummy, who is a gem,

So this, my first poem, is just for them!

Freddie Donnan (4)
Dragonflies, Axminster

41

My First Poem

My name is Harry and I go to preschool,

My best friend is Lucas, who is really cool.

I watch Fireman Sam on TV,

Playing cars is lots of fun for me.

I just love bananas to eat,

And sometimes hot chocolate for a treat.

Blue is a colour I like a lot,

My marble run is the best present I ever got.

My favourite person is Grandad, who is a gem,

So this, my first poem, is just for them!

Harry Beck (4)
Dragonflies, Axminster

My First Poem

My name is Akein and I go to preschool,

My best friend is Shanjayan, who is really cool.

I watch Peppa Pig on TV,

Playing with my train set is lots of fun for me.

I just love bananas to eat,

And sometimes chocolate for a treat.

Brown is a colour I like a lot,

My Fred is the best present I ever got.

My favourite person is Mommy, who is a gem,

So this, my first poem, is just for them!

Akein Nanayakkara (3)
Dragonflies, Axminster

My First Poem

My name is Matilda and I go to preschool,

My best friend is Giles, who is really cool.

I watch Rapunzel on TV,

Playing dolls is lots of fun for me.

I just love pasta to eat,

And sometimes cake for a treat.

Blue is a colour I like a lot,

My tent in my room is the best present I ever got.

My favourite person is Mummy, who is a gem,

So this, my first poem, is just for them!

Matilda Hurford (4)

Dragonflies, Axminster

My First Poem

My name is Kitty and I go to preschool,

My best friend is Rudy, who is really cool.

I watch Frozen on TV,

Playing with my dolls is lots of fun for me.

I just love pasta to eat,

And sometimes chocolate for a treat.

Yellow is a colour I like a lot,

My scooter is the best present I ever got.

My favourite person is Mummy, who is a gem,

So this, my first poem, is just for them!

Kitty Pratt (3)
Dragonflies, Axminster

My First Poem

My name is Roxanne Kathleen and I go to preschool,

My best friend is Logan James, who is really cool.

I watch CBeebies and Tiny Pop on TV,

Playing babies and pushchairs is lots of fun for me.

I just love carrots and strawberries to eat,

And sometimes sweets and crisps for a treat.

Bright purple is a colour I like a lot,

My dog Daisy is the best present I ever got.

My favourite person is Daddy, who is a gem,

So this, my first poem, is just for them!

Roxanne Kathleen Lindsay (2)
Dragonflies, Axminster

My First Poem

My name is Katie and I go to preschool,

My best friend is Shanjayan, who is really cool.

I watch Peppa Pig on TV,

Playing with sand is lots of fun for me.

I just love sandwiches to eat,

And sometimes sweeties for a treat.

Blue is a colour I like a lot,

My Elsa from Frozen is the best present I ever got.

My favourite person is Kayla, who is a gem,

So this, my first poem, is just for them!

Katie Froom (3)
Dragonflies, Axminster

My First Poem

My name is Ruby and I go to preschool,

My best friend is Bluebell, who is really cool.

I watch Woolly and Tig on TV,

Playing with my toys is lots of fun for me.

I just love fish fingers to eat,

And sometimes chocolate for a treat.

Pink is a colour I like a lot,

My princess castle is the best present I ever got.

My favourite person is my nanny, who is a gem,

So this, my first poem, is just for them!

Ruby Farnden (4)

Dragonflies, Axminster

My First Poem

My name is Tilly and I go to preschool,

My best friend is Eva, who is really cool.

I watch Sleeping Beauty on TV,

Playing pushchairs and dolls is lots of fun for me.

I just love apples to eat,

And sometimes sweets for a treat.

Pink is a colour I like a lot,

My babies are the best present I ever got.

My favourite person is Mummy, who is a gem,

So this, my first poem, is just for them!

Matilda Beddows (2)
Dragonflies, Axminster

My First Poem

My name is Max and I go to preschool,

My best friend is Freddie, who is really cool.

I watch Scooby-Doo on TV,

Playing big cars is lots of fun for me.

I just love sausages to eat,

And sometimes sweets for a treat.

Red is a colour I like a lot,

My bike is the best present I ever got.

My favourite person is Daddy, who is a gem,

So this, my first poem, is just for them!

Max Harry Pike (4)
Dragonflies, Axminster

My First Poem

My name is Henri and I go to preschool,

My best friend is Lucas, who is really cool.

I watch Chugginton on TV,

Playing Lightning McQueen is lots of fun for me.

I just love cabbage to eat,

And sometimes cough sweets for a treat.

Blue is a colour I like a lot,

My skipper is the best present I ever got.

My favourite person is Shanjayan, who is a gem,

So this, my first poem, is just for them!

Henri Mcauley (4)
Dragonflies, Axminster

51

My First Poem

My name is Tyler and I go to preschool,

My best friend is Daddy, who is really cool.

I watch McQueen on TV,

Playing cars is lots of fun for me.

I just love tea to eat,

And sometimes chocolate for a treat.

Blue is a colour I like a lot,

My car is the best present I ever got.

My favourite person is Mummy, who is a gem,

So this, my first poem, is just for them!

Tyler John Rainey (2)
Dragonflies, Axminster

My First Poem

My name is Ethan and I go to preschool,

My best friend is Pippa, who is really cool.

I watch Dinosaurs and Transformers on TV,

Playing dinosaurs is lots of fun for me.

I just love sweets and pineapple to eat,

And sometimes ice cream for a treat.

Green is a colour I like a lot,

My trampoline is the best present I ever got.

My favourite person is Pippa, who is a gem,

So this, my first poem, is just for them!

Ethan Prosser (3)
Galmpton Preschool, Brixham

My First Poem

My name is Samuel and I go to preschool,

My best friend is Ashleigh, who is really cool.

I watch Lightning McQueen on TV,

Playing with my engines is lots of fun for me.

I just love peanut butter and waffles to eat,

And sometimes chocolate buttons for a treat.

Light blue is a colour I like a lot,

My Lydham Manor engine is the best present I

ever got.

My favourite person is Mummy, who is a gem,

So this, my first poem, is just for them!

Samuel Emmins (3)
Galmpton Preschool, Brixham

My First Poem

My name is Freya and I go to preschool,

My best friend is Emily, who is really cool.

I watch CBeebies on TV,

Playing in my kitchen is lots of fun for me.

I just love my nana's steak pie to eat,

And sometimes cake and ice cream for a treat.

Purple is a colour I like a lot,

My pink toy car is the best present I ever got.

My favourite person is my sister, Evie, who is a gem,

So this, my first poem, is just for them!

Freya Elise Westaway (2)

Galmpton Preschool, Brixham

My First Poem

My name is Charlie and I go to preschool,

My best friend is Mummy, who is really cool.

I watch football on TV,

Playing with Lego is lots of fun for me.

I just love chocolate to eat,

And sometimes sweets for a treat.

Blue is a colour I like a lot,

My remote controlled car is the best present I

ever got.

My favourite person is Daddy, who is a gem,

So this, my first poem, is just for them!

Charlie Maker (3)
Galmpton Preschool, Brixham

My First Poem

My name is Charlotte and I go to preschool,

My best friend is Aurelie, who is really cool.

I watch Katie Morag on TV,

Playing with my sister is lots of fun for me.

I just love ham and coleslaw to eat,

And sometimes chocolate buttons for a treat.

Pink is a colour I like a lot,

My bike is the best present I ever got.

My favourite person is my daddy, who is a gem,

So this, my first poem, is just for them!

Charlotte Dillistone (4)
Galmpton Preschool, Brixham

My First Poem

My name is Henry-Joe and I go to preschool,

My best friend is Zac, who is really cool.

I watch Thomas the Tank Engine and

Twirlywoos on TV,

Playing dressing up is lots of fun for me.

I just love salmon to eat,

And sometimes a Walnut Whip for a treat.

White is a colour I like a lot,

My Mike the Knight is the best present I ever got.

My favourite person is my brother, George, who is a

gem,

So this, my first poem, is just for them!

Henry-Joe Vale (2)
Galmpton Preschool, Brixham

My First Poem

My name is Eddie and I go to preschool,

My best friend is Ollie, who is really cool.

I watch Fireman Sam on TV,

Playing with my garage is lots of fun for me.

I just love cheese sandwiches to eat,

And sometimes ice cream for a treat.

Blue is a colour I like a lot,

My ride-on digger is the best present I ever got.

My favourite person is Daddy, who is a gem,

So this, my first poem, is just for them!

Edward Thomas Mitchell (2)
Galmpton Preschool, Brixham

59

My First Poem

My name is Amelie and I go to preschool,

My best friend is Jakey, who is really cool.

I watch Peter Rabbit on TV,

Playing with my daddy is lots of fun for me.

I just love ice cream to eat,

And sometimes strawberries for a treat.

Red is a colour I like a lot,

My trampoline is the best present I ever got.

My favourite person is my cousin, Jacob, who is a gem,

So this, my first poem, is just for them!

Amelie Butler (3)
Galmpton Preschool, Brixham

My First Poem

My name is Harry Potter and I go to preschool,

My best friend is Hermione, who is really cool.

I watch Chamber of Secrets on TV,

Playing with Lego is lots of fun for me.

I just love ice cream to eat,

And sometimes chocolate for a treat.

Blue is a colour I like a lot,

My bicycle is the best present I ever got.

My favourite person is Professor McGonagall, who

is a gem,

So this, my first poem, is just for them!

Will Shepperson (4)
Galmpton Preschool, Brixham

61

My First Poem

My name is Boy and I go to preschool,

My best friend is Zak, who is really cool.

I watch Dinosaurs on TV,

Playing football is lots of fun for me.

I just love pasta bake to eat,

And sometimes chocolate Nutella for a treat.

Green is a colour I like a lot,

My Zoomer dinosaur is the best present I ever got.

My favourite person is Nannie, who is a gem,

So this, my first poem, is just for them!

Boy Viktor Furmedge (4)
Galmpton Preschool, Brixham

My First Poem

My name is Ashleigh and I go to preschool,

My best friend is Lily, who is really cool.

I watch Frozen on TV,

Playing with fairies is lots of fun for me.

I just love sausages to eat,

And sometimes ice cream for a treat.

Red is a colour I like a lot,

My Tinkerbell doll is the best present I ever got.

My favourite person is Sofia, my sister, who is a gem,

So this, my first poem, is just for them!

Ashleigh May Green (3)
Galmpton Preschool, Brixham

63

My First Poem

My name is Zachy and I go to preschool,

My best friend is my daddy, who is really cool.

I watch Dinosaurs and Danny MacAskill on TV,

Playing diggers in the dirt is lots of fun for me.

I just love chips to eat,

And sometimes ice cream for a treat.

Green is a colour I like a lot,

My trampoline is the best present I ever got.

My favourite person is my grandad, who is a gem,

So this, my first poem, is just for them!

Zachariah Henry-Lee Turner (2)

Galmpton Preschool, Brixham

My First Poem

My name is Aleka and I go to preschool,

My best friend is Amelie, who is really cool.

I watch Tinkerbell on TV,

Playing and reading is lots of fun for me.

I just love raspberries to eat,

And sometimes sweets for a treat.

Red is a colour I like a lot,

My sister, Nilah, is the best present I ever got.

My favourite person is Nilah, who is a gem,

So this, my first poem, is just for them!

Aleka Sumatpimolchai (3)
Galmpton Preschool, Brixham

My First Poem

My name is Aurelie and I go to preschool,

My best friend is Lily, who is really cool.

I watch Teacup Travels on TV,

Playing princesses is lots of fun for me.

I just love pasta to eat,

And sometimes a sweet for a treat.

Pink is a colour I like a lot,

My bread set is the best present I ever got.

My favourite person is Felix, who is a gem,

So this, my first poem, is just for them!

Aurelie Christopher (4)
Galmpton Preschool, Brixham

My First Poem

My name is Zinnia and I go to preschool,

My best friend is Robyn, who is really cool.

I watch Bubble Guppies on TV,

Playing with babies is lots of fun for me.

I just love cucumber to eat,

And sometimes cupcakes for a treat.

Purple is a colour I like a lot,

My DigiBird is the best present I ever got.

My favourite person is Mummy, who is a gem,

So this, my first poem, is just for them!

Zinnia Smith (4)
Galmpton Preschool, Brixham

67

My First Poem

My name is Reuben and I go to preschool,

My best friend is Thomas, who is really cool.

I watch CBeebies on TV,

Playing outside is lots of fun for me.

I just love sandwiches to eat,

And sometimes sweets for a treat.

Green is a colour I like a lot,

My Spider-Man is the best present I ever got.

My favourite person is Ellie, who is a gem,

So this, my first poem, is just for them!

Reuben Hampshire (2)

Happy Days South West Limited – Treloggan, Newquay

My First Poem

My name is Evan and I go to preschool,

My best friend is Mummy, who is really cool.

I watch Despicable Me on TV,

Playing with diggers is lots of fun for me.

I just love spaghetti Bolognese to eat,

And sometimes chocolate for a treat.

Green is a colour I like a lot,

My Buzz is the best present I ever got.

My favourite person is Daddy, who is a gem,

So this, my first poem, is just for them!

Evan McElroy (4)
Happy Days South West Limited - Treloggan, Newquay

My First Poem

My name is Lily and I go to preschool,

My best friend is Jenna, who is really cool.

I watch Postman Pat on TV,

Playing with my Frozen toys is lots of fun for me.

I just love Marmite to eat,

And sometimes straws for a treat.

Pink is a colour I like a lot,

My big bunny rabbit is the best present I ever got.

My favourite person is Nana, who is a gem,

So this, my first poem, is just for them!

Lily Burrows (3)
Happy Days South West Limited – Treloggan, Newquay

70

My First Poem

My name is Tyler and I go to preschool,

My best friend is Summer, who is really cool.

I watch Fireman Sam on TV,

Playing trains is lots of fun for me.

I just love grapes to eat,

And sometimes broccoli for a treat.

Green is a colour I like a lot,

My big aeroplane is the best present I ever got.

My favourite person is Mummy, who is a gem,

So this, my first poem, is just for them!

Tyler Phillips Linskey (3)
Happy Days South West Limited – Treloggan, Newquay

71

My First Poem

My name is Emily-Jai and I go to preschool,

My best friend is Rhia, who is really cool.

I watch Peppa Pig on TV,

Playing puzzles is lots of fun for me.

I just love toast to eat,

And sometimes Daddy's chocolate for a treat.

Red is a colour I like a lot,

My tablet is the best present I ever got.

My favourite person is Sasha, who is a gem,

So this, my first poem, is just for them!

Emily-Jai Blight (3)

Happy Days South West Limited – Treloggan, Newquay

My First Poem

My name is Joziah and I go to preschool,

My best friend is Alex, who is really cool.

I watch Oscar on TV,

Playing dinosaurs is lots of fun for me.

I just love chicken bagels to eat,

And sometimes ice cream for a treat.

White is a colour I like a lot,

My aeroplane is the best present I ever got.

My favourite person is Finnlay, who is a gem,

So this, my first poem, is just for them!

Joziah Rose-Lean (4)
Happy Days South West Limited - Treloggan, Newquay

My First Poem

My name is Maddie and I go to preschool,

My best friend is Isla, who is really cool.

I watch Dora the Explorer on TV,

Playing with my Barbie dolls is lots of fun for me.

I just love Coco Pops to eat,

And sometimes sweeties and chocolate for a treat.

Purple is a colour I like a lot,

My Barbie car is the best present I ever got.

My favourite person is my mummy, who is a gem,

So this, my first poem, is just for them!

Maddie King (4)
Happy Days South West Limited – Treloggan, Newquay

74

My First Poem

My name is Mia and I go to preschool,

My best friend is Jenna, who is really cool.

I watch music on TV,

Playing with Anna and Elsa dolls is lots of fun for

me.

I just love broccoli to eat,

And sometimes sweets for a treat.

Pink is a colour I like a lot,

My toy is the best present I ever got.

My favourite person is Grandad, who is a gem,

So this, my first poem, is just for them!

Mia Batram (2)
Happy Days South West Limited - Treloggan, Newquay

My First Poem

My name is Jenna and I go to preschool,

My best friend is Millie, who is really cool.

I watch BBC 3 on TV,

Playing puzzles is lots of fun for me.

I just love fish fingers and mash to eat,

And sometimes a chocolate lolly bar for a treat.

Red is a colour I like a lot,

My scooter is the best present I ever got.

My favourite person is Daddy, who is a gem,

So this, my first poem, is just for them!

Jenna Fox (3)
Happy Days South West Limited – Treloggan, Newquay

My First Poem

My name is Lewis and I go to preschool,

My best friend is Oskar, who is really cool.

I watch Garfield on TV,

Playing with the aeroplane toys is lots of fun for

me.

I just love chicken to eat,

And sometimes sweeties for a treat.

Blue is a colour I like a lot,

My train toy is the best present I ever got.

My favourite person is Daddy, who is a gem,

So this, my first poem, is just for them!

Lewis Tyler Purchase (4)
Happy Days South West Limited – Treloggan, Newquay

77

My First Poem

My name is Max and I go to preschool,

My best friend is Savannah, who is really cool.

I watch Thomas on TV,

Playing trains on the computer is lots of fun for

me.

I just love cottage pie to eat,

And sometimes sweets for a treat.

Blue is a colour I like a lot,

My Thomas the Tank Engine is the best present I

ever got.

My favourite person is my mummy, who is a gem,

So this, my first poem, is just for them!

Max Harrison (3)
Happy Days South West Limited – Treloggan, Newquay

My First Poem

My name is Millie and I go to preschool,

My best friend is Jenna, who is really cool.

I watch Pirates on TV,

Playing Connect 4 is lots of fun for me.

I just love salad to eat,

And sometimes gummy bears for a treat.

Pink is a colour I like a lot,

My dolly is the best present I ever got.

My favourite person is Grandad, who is a gem,

So this, my first poem, is just for them!

Millie Wakelam (2)
Happy Days South West Limited - Treloggan, Newquay

My First Poem

My name is Savannah and I go to preschool,

My best friend is Cameron, who is really cool.

I watch Nick Junior on TV,

Playing Jake is lots of fun for me.

I just love bananas to eat,

And sometimes chocolate for a treat.

Blue is a colour I like a lot,

My Jake the pirate toy is the best present I ever got.

My favourite person is Mummy, who is a gem,

So this, my first poem, is just for them!

Savannah Chapman (3)
Happy Days South West Limited – Treloggan, Newquay

My First Poem

My name is Juliet and I go to preschool,

My best friend is Scarlet, who is really cool.

I watch panda bears on TV,

Playing with my sister is lots of fun for me.

I just love carrots to eat,

And sometimes chocolate for a treat.

Purple is a colour I like a lot,

My sister is the best present I ever got.

My favourite person is Mummy, who is a gem,

So this, my first poem, is just for them!

Juliet Pearce (2)
Happy Days South West Limited - Treloggan, Newquay

81

My First Poem

My name is Luna and I go to preschool,

My best friend is Poppy, who is really cool.

I watch Ninja Turtles on TV,

Playing with my balls is lots of fun for me.

I just love pasta to eat,

And sometimes a special yoghurt for a treat.

Yellow is a colour I like a lot,

My cooker is the best present I ever got.

My favourite person is Mummy, who is a gem,

So this, my first poem, is just for them!

Luna Blue Lawrence (3)
Happy Days South West Limited – Treloggan, Newquay

My First Poem

My name is Max and I go to preschool,

My best friend is Ethan, who is really cool.

I watch Thomas the Tank Engine on TV,

Playing diggers is lots of fun for me.

I just love a roast dinner to eat,

And sometimes sweets for a treat.

Blue is a colour I like a lot,

My Thomas the Tank Engine is the best present I

ever got.

My favourite person is Mummy, who is a gem,

So this, my first poem, is just for them!

Max Zolla (3)
Happy Days South West Limited – Treloggan, Newquay

My First Poem

My name is Maja and I go to preschool,

My best friend is Lilly, who is really cool.

I watch Peppa Pig on TV,

Playing with my dolls is lots of fun for me.

I just love chicken soup to eat,

And sometimes ice cream for a treat.

Pink is a colour I like a lot,

My Play-Doh set is the best present I ever got.

My favourite person is Mummy, who is a gem,

So this, my first poem, is just for them!

Maja Abram (3)
Happy Days South West Limited – Treloggan, Newquay

84

My First Poem

My name is Mia and I go to preschool,

My best friend is Lillie, who is really cool.

I watch Frozen on TV,

Playing babies is lots of fun for me.

I just love sandwiches to eat,

And sometimes pink ice cream for a treat.

Green is a colour I like a lot,

My dolly is the best present I ever got.

My favourite person is Daddy, who is a gem,

So this, my first poem, is just for them!

Mia Sawyers (4)
Happy Days South West Limited – Treloggan, Newquay

My First Poem

My name is Rhia-Jae and I go to preschool,

My best friend is Big Lily, who is really cool.

I watch CBeebies on TV,

Playing tickle monsters with my daddy is lots

of fun for me.

I just love spaghetti Bolognese and garlic

bread to eat,

And sometimes sweets for a treat.

Pink is a colour I like a lot,

My scooter is the best present I ever got.

My favourite person is Daddy, who is a gem,

So this, my first poem, is just for them!

Rhia-Jae Marks (3)

Happy Days South West Limited – Treloggan, Newquay

My First Poem

My name is Lillie and I go to preschool,

My best friend is Layla, who is really cool.

I watch Frozen on TV,

Playing with Frozen toys is lots of fun for me.

I just love biscuits to eat,

And sometimes pink ice cream for a treat.

Pink is a colour I like a lot,

My Frozen toy is the best present I ever got.

My favourite person is Mummy, who is a gem,

So this, my first poem, is just for them!

Lillie Stevens (2)

Happy Days South West Limited – Treloggan, Newquay

My First Poem

My name is Jamie and I go to preschool,

My best friend is Oskar, who is really cool.

I watch Mr Tumble on TV,

Playing Thomas is lots of fun for me.

I just love biscuits to eat,

And sometimes chocolate for a treat.

Red is a colour I like a lot,

My Mr Tumble DVD is the best present I ever got.

My favourite person is Dad, who is a gem,

So this, my first poem, is just for them!

Jamie Martin Nile (3)
Happy Days South West Limited – Treloggan, Newquay

My First Poem

My name is Izak and I go to preschool,

My best friend is Marley, who is really cool.

I watch racing cars on TV,

Playing on the slides at the park is lots of fun for

me.

I just love strawberries to eat,

And sometimes chocolate for a treat.

Green is a colour I like a lot,

My car is the best present I ever got.

My favourite person is Zak, who is a gem,

So this, my first poem, is just for them!

Izak Lategan (2)
Happy Days South West Limited – Treloggan, Newquay

My First Poem

My name is Poppy and I go to preschool,

My best friend is Lillie, who is really cool.

I watch CBeebies on TV,

Playing with Lillie is lots of fun for me.

I just love hot dogs to eat,

And sometimes sweets for a treat.

Blue is a colour I like a lot,

My Gruffalo toy is the best present I ever got.

My favourite person is Father Christmas, who is a gem,

So this, my first poem, is just for them!

Poppy White (3)
Happy Days South West Limited – Treloggan, Newquay

My First Poem

My name is Piotr and I go to preschool,

My best friend is Vannessa, who is really cool.

I watch Thomas and Friends on TV,

Playing football is lots of fun for me.

I just love fish fingers to eat,

And sometimes cookies for a treat.

Green is a colour I like a lot,

My police car is the best present I ever got.

My favourite person is Mummy, who is a gem,

So this, my first poem, is just for them!

Piotr Ochman (3)
Happy Days South West Limited - Treloggan, Newquay

My First Poem

My name is Emily and I go to preschool,

My best friend is Phoebe, who is really cool.

I watch Peppa Pig on TV,

Playing cooking is lots of fun for me.

I just love beans on toast and cheese to eat,

And sometimes a lolly for a treat.

Pink is a colour I like a lot,

My Peppa Pig is the best present I ever got.

My favourite person is Max, who is a gem,

So this, my first poem, is just for them!

Emily-Louise Campion (4)
Happy Days South West Limited – Treloggan, Newquay

My First Poem

My name is Buddy and I go to preschool,

My best friend is Savannah, who is really cool.

I watch Mister Maker on TV,

Playing cars is lots of fun for me.

I just love mashed potatoes to eat,

And sometimes chocolate for a treat.

Yellow is a colour I like a lot,

My skateboard is the best present I ever got.

My favourite person is Nanna, who is a gem,

So this, my first poem, is just for them!

Buddy Andrew (3)
Happy Days South West Limited - Treloggan, Newquay

93

My First Poem

My name is Sakara and I go to preschool,

My best friend is my mummy, who is really cool.

I watch Sofia the First on TV,

Playing with my butterfly is lots of fun for me.

I just love pizza to eat,

And sometimes ice cream for a treat.

Black is a colour I like a lot,

My butterfly is the best present I ever got.

My favourite person is Mummy, who is a gem,

So this, my first poem, is just for them!

Sakara-Mai Venner (3)

Happy Days South West Limited – Treloggan, Newquay

94

My First Poem

My name is Zöe and I go to preschool,

My best friend is Amy, who is really cool.

I watch Dumbo on TV,

Playing football is lots of fun for me.

I just love cheese to eat,

And sometimes chocolate for a treat.

Pink is a colour I like a lot,

My Efalunt is the best present I ever got.

My favourite person is Mummy, who is a gem,

So this, my first poem, is just for them!

Zöe Ward (4)
Hartland Preschool, Bideford

My First Poem

My name is Amy and I go to preschool,

My best friend is Caitlin, who is really cool.

I watch Tiny Pop on TV,

Playing with my buggy is lots of fun for me.

I just love carrots to eat,

And sometimes ice cream for a treat.

Yellow is a colour I like a lot,

My doll's buggy is the best present I ever got.

My favourite person is Mummy, who is a gem,

So this, my first poem, is just for them!

Amy Heard (4)
Hartland Preschool, Bideford

My First Poem

My name is Alisha and I go to preschool,

My best friend is Emily, who is really cool.

I watch Frozen on TV,

Playing doctors is lots of fun for me.

I just love bananas to eat,

And sometimes fudge for a treat.

Pink is a colour I like a lot,

My Elsa dolly is the best present I ever got.

My favourite person is Grandad, who is a gem,

So this, my first poem, is just for them!

Alisha Bond (3)
Hartland Preschool, Bideford

My First Poem

My name is James and I go to preschool,

My best friend is Hayley, who is really cool.

I watch I Can Cook on TV,

Playing on my bike is lots of fun for me.

I just love cheese sandwiches to eat,

And sometimes a ginger nut for a treat.

Green is a colour I like a lot,

My remote control digger is the best present I

ever got.

My favourite person is Nan, who is a gem,

So this, my first poem, is just for them!

James Benn (3)
Hartland Preschool, Bideford

My First Poem

My name is Tommy and I go to preschool,

My best friend is Harry, who is really cool.

I watch Bing on TV,

Playing cars is lots of fun for me.

I just love meatballs and pasta to eat,

And sometimes sweets for a treat.

Purple is a colour I like a lot,

My bike is the best present I ever got.

My favourite person is Mummy, who is a gem,

So this, my first poem, is just for them!

Tommy Thorne (3)
Hartland Preschool, Bideford

My First Poem

My name is Jack and I go to preschool,

My best friend is Evie , who is really cool.

I watch Fireman Sam on TV,

Playing Marble Run is lots of fun for me.

I just love fruit and pasta to eat,

And sometimes chocolate for a treat.

Red is a colour I like a lot,

My Scalextric is the best present I ever got.

My favourite person is Aunty Mich, who is a gem,

So this, my first poem, is just for them!

Jack Stubbs (4)
Hartland Preschool, Bideford

My First Poem

My name is Rory and I go to preschool,

My best friend is George, who is really cool.

I watch Ben and Holly on TV,

Playing with my blocks is lots of fun for me.

I just love beans on toast to eat,

And sometimes chocolate for a treat.

Blue is a colour I like a lot,

My giant dinosaur is the best present I ever got.

My favourite person is my big brother, George, who

is a gem,

So this, my first poem, is just for them!

Rory Vanstone (2)
Hartland Preschool, Bideford

101

My First Poem

My name is George and I go to preschool,

My best friend is Rory, who is really cool.

I watch Spider-Man on TV,

Playing omnom is lots of fun for me.

I just love pasta and sweetcorn to eat,

And sometimes ice cream for a treat.

Blue is a colour I like a lot,

My giant robot is the best present I ever got.

My favourite person is my little brother, Rory, who

is a gem,

So this, my first poem, is just for them!

George Vanstone (4)

Hartland Preschool, Bideford

My First Poem

My name is Sophia and I go to preschool,

My best friend is Mary, who is really cool.

I watch Sofia the First on TV,

Playing in the park is lots of fun for me.

I just love chicken nuggets and wedges to eat,

And sometimes chocolate for a treat.

Blue is a colour I like a lot,

My mermail is the best present I ever got.

My favourite person is Daddy, who is a gem,

So this, my first poem, is just for them!

Sophia Wynne Jarvis (3)
Hartland Preschool, Bideford

My First Poem

My name is Holly and I go to preschool,

My best friend is Emily, who is really cool.

I watch Frozen on TV,

Playing with dolls is lots of fun for me.

I just love egg sandwiches to eat,

And sometimes sweets for a treat.

Purple is a colour I like a lot,

My ride-on car is the best present I ever got.

My favourite person is Mummy, who is a gem,

So this, my first poem, is just for them!

Holly Heard (4)
Hartland Preschool, Bideford

My First Poem

My name is Emily and I go to preschool,

My best friend is Alisha, who is really cool.

I watch Peppa Pig on TV,

Playing with my jigsaw is lots of fun for me.

I just love lots of fruit to eat,

And sometimes a Kinder Surprise for a treat.

Pink is a colour I like a lot,

My My Little Pony is the best present I ever got.

My favourite person is Mummy, who is a gem,

So this, my first poem, is just for them!

Emily Keene (4)
Hartland Preschool, Bideford

My First Poem

My name is Shane and I go to preschool,

My best friend is Ashleigh, who is really cool.

I watch SpongeBob SquarePants on TV,

Playing football is lots of fun for me.

I just love carrots and biscuits to eat,

And sometimes cake for a treat.

Green is a colour I like a lot,

My tractor is the best present I ever got.

My favourite person is Dad, who is a gem,

So this, my first poem, is just for them!

Shane Cornish (3)
Hartland Preschool, Bideford

My First Poem

My name is Amy and I go to preschool,

My best friend is Alice, who is really cool.

I watch Peter Rabbit on TV,

Playing hide-and-seek is lots of fun for me.

I just love sausages to eat,

And sometimes sweets for a treat.

Yellow is a colour I like a lot,

My toy elephant is the best present I ever got.

My favourite person is Mummy, who is a gem,

So this, my first poem, is just for them!

Amy Thorne (4)
Hartland Preschool, Bideford

My First Poem

My name is Rhys and I go to preschool,

My best friend is Ben, who is really cool.

I watch PAW Patrol on TV,

Playing with my tractor and diggers is lots of

fun for me.

I just love pizza to eat,

And sometimes I have chocolate buttons for a

treat.

Green is a colour I like a lot,

My John Deere tractor is the best present I ever

got.

My favourite person is Mummy, who is a gem,

So this, my first poem, is just for them!

Rhys Cornish (4)
Hartland Preschool, Bideford

My First Poem

My name is Aaron and I go to preschool,

My best friend is Rhys, who is really cool.

I watch Tractor Ted on TV,

Playing with my digger is lots of fun for me.

I just love bacon to eat,

And sometimes I have Haribos for a treat.

Blue is a colour I like a lot,

My blue tractor is the best present I ever got.

My favourite person is Daddy, who is a gem,

So this, my first poem, is just for them!

Aaron Cornish (3)
Hartland Preschool, Bideford

My First Poem

My name is Ronnie and I go to preschool,

My best friend is Reece, who is really cool.

I watch Mr Jean on TV,

Playing football is lots of fun for me.

I just love chips to eat,

And sometimes chocolate cake for a treat.

Blue is a colour I like a lot,

My racing track car is the best present I ever got.

My favourite person is Sophia, who is a gem,

So this, my first poem, is just for them!

Ronnie Whapham (4)
Hartland Preschool, Bideford

My First Poem

My name is Jamie and I go to preschool,

My best friend is James, who is really cool.

I watch Fireman Sam on TV,

Playing cars is lots of fun for me.

I just love pizza to eat,

And sometimes chocolate cake for a treat.

Blue is a colour I like a lot,

My LeapPad 3 is the best present I ever got.

My favourite person is Mummy, who is a gem,

So this, my first poem, is just for them!

Jamie Monk (3)
Hartland Preschool, Bideford

III

My First Poem

My name is Jack and I go to preschool,

My best friend is Jago, who is really cool.

I watch CBeebies on TV,

Playing Fireman Sam is lots of fun for me.

I just love Nannie's roast to eat,

And sometimes chocolate bars for a treat.

Red is a colour I like a lot,

My racing car is the best present I ever got.

My favourite person is Fleur, who is a gem,

So this, my first poem, is just for them!

Jack Laban (3)
Helston Day Nursery, Helston

My First Poem

My name is Jayden and I go to preschool,

My best friend is Alana, who is really cool.

I watch Sailor Sid on TV,

Playing cars is lots of fun for me.

I just love pasta to eat,

And sometimes orange for a treat.

Red is a colour I like a lot,

My dinosaur game is the best present I ever got.

My favourite person is Jago, who is a gem,

So this, my first poem, is just for them!

Jayden Duffield (3)
Helston Day Nursery, Helston

My First Poem

My name is Emma and I go to preschool,

My best friend is Izzy, who is really cool.

I watch Chitty Chitty Bang Bang on TV,

Playing builders is lots of fun for me.

I just love pretzels to eat,

And sometimes biscuits for a treat.

Pink is a colour I like a lot,

My Elsa singing doll is the best present I ever got.

My favourite person is Mummy, who is a gem,

So this, my first poem, is just for them!

Emma Kenyon (3)
Helston Day Nursery, Helston

My First Poem

My name is Izzy and I go to preschool,

My best friend is my mum, who is really cool.

I watch The Little Mermaid on TV,

Playing with my teddy is lots of fun for me.

I just love lollies to eat,

And sometimes sweets for a treat.

Purple is a colour I like a lot,

My yo-yo is the best present I ever got.

My favourite person is my mum, who is a gem,

So this, my first poem, is just for them!

Izzy Stuteley (4)
Helston Day Nursery, Helston

My First Poem

My name is Jago and I go to preschool,

My best friend is Jacob, who is really cool.

I watch Hey Dog on TV,

Playing digger is lots of fun for me.

I just love pasta to eat,

And sometimes chocolate for a treat.

Green is a colour I like a lot,

My Transformer is the best present I ever got.

My favourite person is Kai, who is a gem,

So this, my first poem, is just for them!

Jago Hoskin (4)
Helston Day Nursery, Helston

My First Poem

My name is Finley and I go to preschool,

My best friend is Jayden, who is really cool.

I watch The Incredibles on TV,

Playing my new train is lots of fun for me.

I just love biscuits to eat,

And sometimes chocolates for a treat.

Blue is a colour I like a lot,

My new train is the best present I ever got.

My favourite person is Miles, who is a gem,

So this, my first poem, is just for them!

Finley Wallens-Hancock (3)
Helston Day Nursery, Helston

My First Poem

My name is Agnes and I go to preschool,

My best friend is Ruan, who is really cool.

I watch Peppa Pig on TV,

Playing with my teddies is lots of fun for me.

I just love fruit to eat,

And sometimes jelly for a treat.

Red is a colour I like a lot,

My radio is the best present I ever got.

My favourite person is Daddy, who is a gem,

So this, my first poem, is just for them!

Agnes Coad (3)
Helston Day Nursery, Helston

My First Poem

My name is Callum and I go to preschool,

My best friend is Izzy, who is really cool.

I watch The Gruffalo's Child on TV,

Playing Fireman Sam is lots of fun for me.

I just love pasta to eat,

And sometimes fruit for a treat.

Blue is a colour I like a lot,

My helicopter is the best present I ever got.

My favourite person is Emma, who is a gem,

So this, my first poem, is just for them!

Callum Wilson (3)
Helston Day Nursery, Helston

My First Poem

My name is Sienna and I go to preschool,

My best friend is Evie, who is really cool.

I watch Peppa Pig on TV,

Playing with the kitchen is lots of fun for me.

I just love cucumber to eat,

And sometimes sandwiches for a treat.

Blue is a colour I like a lot,

My Minion is the best present I ever got.

My favourite person is Mummy, who is a gem,

So this, my first poem, is just for them!

Sienna Pollard (3)
Helston Day Nursery, Helston

My First Poem

My name is Alana and I go to preschool,

My best friend is Jago, who is really cool.

I watch The Gruffalo on TV,

Playing with baby Moo Moo in my house is lots

of fun for me.

I just love chips to eat,

And sometimes a yoghurt for a treat.

Pink is a colour I like a lot,

My Dave Dragon is the best present I ever got.

My favourite person is Finley, who is a gem,

So this, my first poem, is just for them!

Alana Mae Bliss (3)
Helston Day Nursery, Helston

My First Poem

My name is Harry and I go to preschool,

My best friend is Sam, who is really cool.

I watch Octonauts on TV,

Playing Transformers is lots of fun for me.

I just love fish fingers, chippies and tomato

sauce to eat,

And sometimes purple juice, Smarties and

yoghurt for a treat.

Black is a colour I like a lot,

My Smokey the fire engine is the best present I

ever got.

My favourite person is Charlie, who is a gem,

So this, my first poem, is just for them!

Harry Dingle (4)
Humpty Dumpty Childcare, Dartmouth

My First Poem

My name is Joshua and I go to preschool,

My best friend is Liam, who is really cool.

I watch Adventure Time on TV,

Playing with my kitten, Boo is lots of fun for me.

I just love baked beans and sausages to eat,

And sometimes sugary sweets for a treat.

Red is a colour I like a lot,

My scary dinosaur is the best present I ever got.

My favourite person is Mummy, who is a gem,

So this, my first poem, is just for them!

Joshua Charles Evan Cooper (4)
Humpty Dumpty Childcare, Dartmouth

My First Poem

My name is Nathan and I go to preschool,

My best friend is Charlie, who is really cool.

I watch Lightning McQueen on TV,

Playing the food game at my house is lots of fun

for me.

I just love spaghetti and cheese to eat,

And sometimes strawberry and chocolate ice

cream for a treat.

Blue is a colour I like a lot,

My Fiery Flynn the fire engine is the best present

I ever got.

My favourite person is Mummy, who is a gem,

So this, my first poem, is just for them!

Nathan Phillips (3)
Humpty Dumpty Childcare, Dartmouth

My First Poem

My name is Sam and I go to preschool,

My best friend is Thomas, who is really cool.

I watch Postman Pat on TV,

Playing cars and trains is lots of fun for me.

I just love apples to eat,

And sometimes chocolate for a treat.

Red is a colour I like a lot,

My toy police car is the best present I ever got.

My favourite person is Mummy, who is a gem,

So this, my first poem, is just for them!

Sam Tier (3)
Humpty Dumpty Childcare, Dartmouth

125

My First Poem

My name is Hugo and I go to preschool,

My best friend is Elsa, who is really cool.

I watch Peppa Pig on TV,

Playing Pegga Pig numbers is lots of fun for me.

I just love chips and apples to eat,

And sometimes cake and ice cream for a treat.

Green is a colour I like a lot,

My little Gruffalo is the best present I ever got.

My favourite person is Felix, the baby, who is a gem,

So this, my first poem, is just for them!

Hugo Harris (3)
Humpty Dumpty Childcare, Dartmouth

My First Poem

My name is Ella and I go to preschool,

My best friend is Isabelle, who is really cool.

I watch Sofia the First on TV,

Playing Tinkerbell puzzles is lots of fun for me.

I just love chips, sauce and peas to eat,

And sometimes chocolate and strawberry ice cream for a treat.

Orange is a colour I like a lot,

My cloth for bath and shower time is the best present I ever got.

My favourite person is Max, who is a gem,

So this, my first poem, is just for them!

Ella Walker (2)
Humpty Dumpty Childcare, Dartmouth

My First Poem

My name is Molly and I go to preschool,
My best friend is Elsa, who is really cool.
I watch Peppa Pig on TV,
Playing bikes is lots of fun for me.
I just love bananas to eat,
And sometimes pineapple for a treat.
Pink is a colour I like a lot,
My pink and purple toy is the best present I ever got.
My favourite person is Mummy, who is a gem,
So this, my first poem, is just for them!

Molly Fontaine Caunter (3)
Humpty Dumpty Childcare, Dartmouth

My First Poem

My name is Matthew and I go to preschool,

My best friend is Sophie, who is really cool.

I watch Fireman Sam on TV,

Playing trains is lots of fun for me.

I just love cheese to eat,

And sometimes biscuits and cake for a treat.

Red is a colour I like a lot,

My pencil set is the best present I ever got.

My favourite person is Daddy, who is a gem,

So this, my first poem, is just for them!

Matthew Wellby (3)
Humpty Dumpty Childcare, Dartmouth

My First Poem

My name is Toby and I go to preschool,

My best friend is Zach, who is really cool.

I watch Thomas The Tank Engine on TV,

Playing puzzle games on DVD is lots of fun for me.

I just love spaghetti and cheese to eat,

And sometimes big chocolate eggs for a treat.

Yellow is a colour I like a lot,

My cuddly, teddy reindeer is the best present I

ever got.

My favourite person is Mummy, who is a gem,

So this, my first poem, is just for them!

Toby Redshaw (3)
Humpty Dumpty Childcare, Dartmouth

My First Poem

My name is Isabelle and I go to preschool,

My best friend is Finley, who is really cool.

I watch Peppa Pig on TV,

Playing dollies with my pram is lots of fun for me.

I just love tomato and broccoli pasta to eat,

And sometimes jelly and ice cream for a treat.

Purple is a colour I like a lot,

My Peppa Pig is the best present I ever got.

My favourite person is Finley, who is a gem,

So this, my first poem, is just for them!

Isabelle Rawlings (3)
Humpty Dumpty Childcare, Dartmouth

131

My First Poem

My name is Finley and I go to preschool,

My best friend is Daddy, who is really cool.

I watch Peppa Pig on TV,

Playing aeroplanes and trains is lots of fun for

me.

I just love barbecue sausages to eat,

And sometimes Weetabix and honey for a treat.

Red is a colour I like a lot,

My very fast fire engine is the best present I ever

got.

My favourite person is Daddy, who is a gem,

So this, my first poem, is just for them!

Finley Rawlings (3)
Humpty Dumpty Childcare, Dartmouth

My First Poem

My name is Dylan and I go to preschool,

My best friend is Kayden, who is really cool.

I watch cartoons on TV,

Playing with my fire engine is lots of fun for me.

I just love chicken to eat,

And sometimes chocolate for a treat.

Yellow is a colour I like a lot,

My lorry is the best present I ever got.

My favourite person is Freddie-Joe, who is a gem,

So this, my first poem, is just for them!

Dylan James Hendin (4)
Humpty Dumpty Childcare, Dartmouth

133

My First Poem

My name is Amira and I go to preschool,

My best friend is Ebony, who is really cool.

I watch Peppa Pig and scary films on TV,

Playing prams and babies is lots of fun for me.

I just love pasta, sauce and cheese to eat,

And sometimes Frozen - Let It Go chocolate for

a treat.

Pink is a colour I like a lot,

My pink pram is the best present I ever got.

My favourite person is Elsa, who is a gem,

So this, my first poem, is just for them!

Amira Panesar (3)
Humpty Dumpty Childcare, Dartmouth

My First Poem

My name is Henry and I go to preschool,

My best friend is Seb, who is really cool.

I watch Fireman Sam on TV,

Playing bikes in the garden is lots of fun for me.

I just love fish and chips to eat,

And sometimes chocolate biscuits for a treat.

Yellow is a colour I like a lot,

My shopping game is the best present I ever got.

My favourite person is Mummy, who is a gem,

So this, my first poem, is just for them!

Henry Notley (2)
Humpty Dumpty Childcare, Dartmouth

My First Poem

My name is Keegan and I go to preschool,

My best friend is Scarlett, who is really cool.

I watch Spider-Man on TV,

Playing in the sand is lots of fun for me.

I just love fish and crisps to eat,

And sometimes blue ice cream for a treat.

Blue is a colour I like a lot,

My big bike is the best present I ever got.

My favourite person is Daddy, who is a gem,

So this, my first poem, is just for them!

Keegan David Hendin (2)
Humpty Dumpty Childcare, Dartmouth

My First Poem

My name is Scarlett-Rose and I go to preschool,

My best friend is Keegan, who is really cool.

I watch Mr Tumble on TV,

Playing egg and spoon is lots of fun for me.

I just love pizza to eat,

And sometimes chocolate cake for a treat.

Blue is a colour I like a lot,

My dolly is the best present I ever got.

My favourite person is Kayden, who is a gem,

So this, my first poem, is just for them!

Scarlett-Rose Hosking (2)
Humpty Dumpty Childcare, Dartmouth

My First Poem

My name is Toby and I go to preschool,

My best friend is Ben , who is really cool.

I watch Spider-Man on TV,

Playing hide-and-seek with my grandma is lots

of fun for me.

I just love fish pie to eat,

And sometimes chocolate cake for a treat.

Yellow is a colour I like a lot,

My truck is the best present I ever got.

My favourite person is Tirian , who is a gem,

So this, my first poem, is just for them!

Toby Bowtell-Stenning (3)
Kingfisher Preschool (Kingsand), Tor Point

My First Poem

My name is Lauren Grace and I go to preschool,

My best friend is Romily, who is really cool.

I watch Let's Play on TV,

Playing with my big brother, James, is lots of fun

for me.

I just love spaghetti Bolognese to eat,

And sometimes chocolate cake for a treat.

Pink is a colour I like a lot,

My Playmobil is the best present I ever got.

My favourite person is Mummy, who is a gem,

So this, my first poem, is just for them!

Lauren Grace Saunders (3)
Kingfisher Preschool (Kingsand), Tor Point

My First Poem

My name is Phoebe and I go to preschool,

My best friend is my brother, Felix, who is really cool.

I watch Kerwhizz on TV,

Playing with water on a hot day is lots of fun for

me.

I just love tube pasta to eat,

And sometimes television for a treat.

Yellow is a colour I like a lot,

My pink bike is the best present I ever got.

My favourite person is little Thomas, who is a gem,

So this, my first poem, is just for them!

Phoebe Jordon (3)
Kingfisher Preschool (Kingsand), Tor Point

My First Poem

My name is Theo and I go to preschool,

My best friend is my brother, who is really cool.

I watch Octonauts on TV,

Playing with Mummy and Daddy is lots of fun for

me.

I just love tomato pizza to eat,

And sometimes cake for a treat.

Green is a colour I like a lot,

My bike is the best present I ever got.

My favourite person is Mummy, who is a gem,

So this, my first poem, is just for them!

Theo Schmid (2)
Kingfisher Preschool (Kingsand), Tor Point

141

My First Poem

My name is Esmé and I go to preschool,

My best friend is Vinny Polak, who is really cool.

I watch Dora the Explorer on TV,

Playing Cooper Cat is lots of fun for me.

I just love monkey nuts to eat,

And sometimes chocolate for a treat.

Blue is a colour I like a lot,

My Elsa dress is the best present I ever got.

My favourite person is Dadda, who is a gem,

So this, my first poem, is just for them!

Esmé Gibbens (4)
Kingfisher Preschool (Kingsand), Tor Point

My First Poem

My name is Romily and I go to preschool,

My best friend is Samson, who is really cool.

I watch Octonauts on TV,

Playing Wild Kratts is lots of fun for me.

I just love slugs to eat,

And sometimes slug pie for a treat.

Purple is a colour I like a lot,

My bike is the best present I ever got.

My favourite person is Squeek, who is a gem,

So this, my first poem, is just for them!

Romily Braun (4)
Kingfisher Preschool (Kingsand), Tor Point

My First Poem

My name is Connor and I go to preschool,

My best friend is Mummy, who is really cool.

I watch SpongeBob on TV,

Playing Hot Wheels games is lots of fun for me.

I just love toast to eat,

And sometimes birthday cake for a treat.

Blue is a colour I like a lot,

My football is the best present I ever got.

My favourite person is Mum, who is a gem,

So this, my first poem, is just for them!

Connor Williams (4)

Kingwood Childcare, Cullompton

My First Poem

My name is William and I go to preschool,

My best friend is Mikey, who is really cool.

I watch Octonauts on TV,

Playing trains is lots of fun for me.

I just love banana to eat,

And sometimes chips for a treat.

Blue is a colour I like a lot,

My Ninja Turtle is the best present I ever got.

My favourite person is Mikey, who is a gem,

So this, my first poem, is just for them!

William Brookes (4)
Kingwood Childcare, Cullompton

My First Poem

My name is Alice and I go to preschool,

My best friend is Flora, who is really cool.

I watch The Simpsons on TV,

Playing games is lots of fun for me.

I just love ham and cheese to eat,

And sometimes sweeties for a treat.

Pink is a colour I like a lot,

My fan is the best present I ever got.

My favourite person is Max, who is a gem,

So this, my first poem, is just for them!

Alice Jennifer Jackson (3)
Kingwood Childcare, Cullompton

My First Poem

My name is Charlie and I go to preschool,

My best friend is Edward, who is really cool.

I watch Gigglebiz on TV,

Playing dogs is lots of fun for me.

I just love sweets to eat,

And sometimes yoghurt for a treat.

Green is a colour I like a lot,

My motorcycle is the best present I ever got.

My favourite person is Mummy, who is a gem,

So this, my first poem, is just for them!

Charlie Samuels (4)
Kingwood Childcare, Cullompton

147

My First Poem

My name is Leon and I go to preschool,

My best friend is Imogen, who is really cool.

I watch Tom and Jerry on TV,

Playing shops is lots of fun for me.

I just love pasta to eat,

And sometimes chocolate for a treat.

Blue is a colour I like a lot,

My alien egg with slime is the best present I ever got.

My favourite person is Kaka, who is a gem,

So this, my first poem, is just for them!

Leon Sanders (3)
Kingwood Childcare, Cullompton

My First Poem

My name is Flora and I go to preschool,

My best friend is Imogen, who is really cool.

I watch Octonauts on TV,

Playing princesses is lots of fun for me.

I just love cheese and potato to eat,

And sometimes sweeties for a treat.

Pink is a colour I like a lot,

My pink and blue bike is the best present I ever got.

My favourite person is Rafferty, who is a gem,

So this, my first poem, is just for them!

Flora Copland (3)

Kingwood Childcare, Cullompton

My First Poem

My name is Imogen and I go to preschool,

My best friend is Evie, who is really cool.

I watch Frozen on TV,

Playing horse games is lots of fun for me.

I just love a baguette to eat,

And sometimes lollipops for a treat.

Purple is a colour I like a lot,

My car is the best present I ever got.

My favourite person is Elsa, who is a gem,

So this, my first poem, is just for them!

Imogen Heathcock (4)
Kingwood Childcare, Cullompton

My First Poem

My name is Gabriel and I go to preschool,

My best friend is Samuel, who is really cool.

I watch Chitty Chitty Bang Bang on TV,

Playing hide-and-seek is lots of fun for me.

I just love cottage pie to eat,

And sometimes chocolate for a treat.

Pink is a colour I like a lot,

My horse, Run Faster, is the best present I ever got.

My favourite person is Granny, who is a gem,

So this, my first poem, is just for them!

Gabriel Sykes (4)
Kingwood Childcare, Cullompton

My First Poem

My name is Alice and I go to preschool,

My best friend is Alice, who is really cool.

I watch Frozen on TV,

Playing car games is lots of fun for me.

I just love sausage and mash to eat,

And sometimes satsumas for a treat.

Red is a colour I like a lot,

My Elsa is the best present I ever got.

My favourite person is Mummy, who is a gem,

So this, my first poem, is just for them!

Alice Hodge (4)
Kingwood Childcare, Cullompton

My First Poem

My name is Archer and I go to preschool,

My best friend is Ben, who is really cool.

I watch Bing on TV,

Playing with puzzles is lots of fun for me.

I just love fish pie to eat,

And sometimes sweeties for a treat.

Red is a colour I like a lot,

My bike is the best present I ever got.

My favourite person is Jack, who is a gem,

So this, my first poem, is just for them!

Archer Steer (3)
Lee Mill Preschool Playgroup, Ivybridge

My First Poem

My name is Isla and I go to preschool,

My best friend is Mia, who is really cool.

I watch PAW Patrol on TV,

Playing with dolls is lots of fun for me.

I just love chips to eat,

And sometimes chocolate for a treat.

Purple is a colour I like a lot,

My pair of shoes is the best present I ever got.

My favourite person is Tristan, who is a gem,

So this, my first poem, is just for them!

Isla Wills (4)
Lee Mill Preschool Playgroup, Ivybridge

My First Poem

My name is Maizy and I go to preschool,

My best friend is Isla, who is really cool.

I watch Scooby-Doo on TV,

Playing on the trampoline is lots of fun for me.

I just love Daddy's chips to eat,

And sometimes candyfloss for a treat.

Red is a colour I like a lot,

My kitchen is the best present I ever got.

My favourite person is Kieron, who is a gem,

So this, my first poem, is just for them!

Maizy Jayne Cameron (4)
Lee Mill Preschool Playgroup, Ivybridge

My First Poem

My name is Tori and I go to preschool,

My best friend is Maizie, who is really cool.

I watch The Simpsons on TV,

Playing dollies with Isla, Maizie and Max is lots

of fun for me.

I just love ham sandwiches to eat,

And sometimes cake for a treat.

Pink is a colour I like a lot,

My dolly is the best present I ever got.

My favourite person is Daddy, who is a gem,

So this, my first poem, is just for them!

Victoria Kerswell (3)
Lee Mill Preschool Playgroup, Ivybridge

My First Poem

My name is Max and I go to preschool,

My best friend is Tori, who is really cool.

I watch PAW Patrol on TV,

Playing with trains and cars is lots of fun for me.

I just love stinky cheese to eat,

And sometimes strawberries for a treat.

Grey is a colour I like a lot,

My train track from Grandad is the best present

I ever got.

My favourite person is Grandad, who is a gem,

So this, my first poem, is just for them!

Max Welsh (4)
Lee Mill Preschool Playgroup, Ivybridge

My First Poem

My name is Nikoletta and I go to preschool,

My best friend is Maizy, who is really cool.

I watch Dora Meets the Word on TV,

Playing football and peekaboo is lots of fun for me.

I just love dumplings with cheese and curry and rice to eat,

And sometimes Daddy for a treat.

Pink is a colour I like a lot,

My game is the best present I ever got.

My favourite person is Daddy, who is a gem,

So this, my first poem, is just for them!

Nikoletta Jez (4)
Lee Mill Preschool Playgroup, Ivybridge

My First Poem

My name is Mia and I go to preschool,

My best friend is Lillie, who is really cool.

I watch Frozen on TV,

Playing marbles is lots of fun for me.

I just love tomatoes to eat,

And sometimes cake for a treat.

Pink is a colour I like a lot,

My My Little Pony is the best present I ever got.

My favourite person is Olivia, who is a gem,

So this, my first poem, is just for them!

Mia Osborne (4)
Lee Mill Preschool Playgroup, Ivybridge

My First Poem

My name is Billy and I go to preschool,

My best friend is Emily, who is really cool.

I watch Gigglebiz on TV,

Playing with my kitchen is lots of fun for me.

I just love ham and cucumber sandwiches to

eat,

And sometimes Magic Stars for a treat.

Blue is a colour I like a lot,

My yellow spotty bag is the best present I ever got.

My favourite person is my baby brother, Henry,

who is a gem,

So this, my first poem, is just for them!

Billy Wilson (2)
Lee Mill Preschool Playgroup, Ivybridge

My First Poem

My name is Jessica and I go to preschool,

My best friend is Maxi Boo Boo, who is really cool.

I watch Frozen on TV,

Playing with my toys is lots of fun for me.

I just love pizza to eat,

And sometimes chocolate for a treat.

Pink is a colour I like a lot,

My Doc McStuffins toy is the best present I ever

got.

My favourite person is Lelly, who is a gem,

So this, my first poem, is just for them!

Jessica Burrage (4)
Nutkins Preschool, Plymouth

 # My First Poem

My name is Charlie and I go to preschool,

My best friend is Erin, who is really cool.

I watch Teenage Mutant Ninja Turtles on TV,

Playing football with my daddy is lots of fun for me.

I just love cheese and tomato pizza to eat,

And sometimes scrummy chocolate for a treat.

Plymouth Argyle green is a colour I like a lot,

My Play-Doh truck is the best present I ever got.

My favourite person is Mummy, who is a gem,

So this, my first poem, is just for them!

Charlie Bond (4)
Nutkins Preschool, Plymouth

My First Poem

My name is Owen and I go to preschool,

My best friend is Great Gran, who is really cool.

I watch Toy Story on TV,

Playing with Buzz and Woody is lots of fun for me.

I just love sausage rolls to eat,

And sometimes Jaffa Cakes for a treat.

Blue is a colour I like a lot,

My Rex dinosaur is the best present I ever got.

My favourite person is Millie, who is a gem,

So this, my first poem, is just for them!

Owen Balston (3)
Pinhoe Preschool, Exeter

163

My First Poem

My name is Zoe and I go to preschool,

My best friend is Ashia, who is really cool.

I watch Peter Rabbit on TV,

Playing with Play-Doh is lots of fun for me.

I just love cheese, potatoes and raisins to eat,

And sometimes chocolate for a treat.

Pink is a colour I like a lot,

My teddy is the best present I ever got.

My favourite person is Great Gran, who is a gem,

So this, my first poem, is just for them!

Zoe Ann Clarkson (4)

Pinhoe Preschool, Exeter

My First Poem

My name is Zachary and I go to preschool,

My best friend is Rhys, who is really cool.

I watch Peppa Pig and Thomas the Tank Engine on TV,

Playing with trains, cars, Lego and Play-Doh is lots of fun for me.

I just love rice, cottage pie, pizza and roast to eat,

And sometimes a Kinder Surprise egg for a treat.

Red is a colour I like a lot,

My train is the best present I ever got.

My favourite person is Mummy, who is a gem,

So this, my first poem, is just for them!

Zachary Underhill (3)
Pinhoe Preschool, Exeter

My First Poem

My name is Hollie and I go to preschool,

My best friend is Willow, who is really cool.

I watch Disney Junior on TV,

Playing Toy Story games is lots of fun for me.

I just love spaghetti Bolognese to eat,

And sometimes a chocolate bunny for a treat.

Pink is a colour I like a lot,

My Lucy Lou is the best present I ever got.

My favourite person is Mummy, who is a gem,

So this, my first poem, is just for them!

Hollie Walkey (3)

Pinhoe Preschool, Exeter

My First Poem

My name is Dylan and I go to preschool,

My best friend is my big brother, Riley, who is really cool.

I watch Henry on TV,

Playing with cars is lots of fun for me.

I just love yummy biscuits to eat,

And sometimes sweeties for a treat.

Blue is a colour I like a lot,

My Buzz Lightyear is the best present I ever got.

My favourite person is my brother, who is a gem,

So this, my first poem, is just for them!

Dylan Budd (2)
Pinhoe Preschool, Exeter

My First Poem

My name is Riley and I go to preschool,

My best friend is Charlie, who is really cool.

I watch Power Rangers on TV,

Playing driving cars is lots of fun for me.

I just love crisps to eat,

And sometimes special sweets for a treat.

Blue is a colour I like a lot,

My silver ranger key with box is the best present

I ever got.

My favourite person is Ben, who is a gem,

So this, my first poem, is just for them!

Riley Budd (4)
Pinhoe Preschool, Exeter

My First Poem

My name is Lola and I go to preschool,

My best friend is Leon, who is really cool.

I watch Ben and Holly on TV,

Playing with my Duplo is lots of fun for me.

I just love strawberries to eat,

And sometimes fizzy sweets for a treat.

Red is a colour I like a lot,

My unicorn is the best present I ever got.

My favourite person is Mummy, who is a gem,

So this, my first poem, is just for them!

Lola Smiles (2)
Pinhoe Preschool, Exeter

169

My First Poem

My name is Callum and I go to preschool,

My best friend is Riley, who is really cool.

I watch cartoons and Boomerang on TV,

Playing with my dinosaurs is lots of fun for me.

I just love ham and cheese sandwiches to eat,

And sometimes sweets for a treat.

Green is a colour I like a lot,

My big dinosaur is the best present I ever got.

My favourite person is Mummy, who is a gem,

So this, my first poem, is just for them!

Callum Price (3)
Pinhoe Preschool, Exeter

My First Poem

My name is Jessica and I go to preschool,

My best friend is Imogen, who is really cool.

I watch Peppa Pig on TV,

Playing hide-and-seek is lots of fun for me.

I just love fish and chips to eat,

And sometimes ice cream for a treat.

Blue is a colour I like a lot,

My Woody is the best present I ever got.

My favourite person is Ellie, my sister, who is a gem,

So this, my first poem, is just for them!

Jessica Lily Clark (4)
Pinhoe Preschool, Exeter

My First Poem

My name is Reegan and I go to preschool,

My best friend is Leon, who is really cool.

I watch PAW Patrol on TV,

Playing with cars is lots of fun for me.

I just love sausages to eat,

And sometimes chocolate for a treat.

Red is a colour I like a lot,

My race track is the best present I ever got.

My favourite person is Daddy, who is a gem,

So this, my first poem, is just for them!

Reegan Balston (3)
Pinhoe Preschool, Exeter

My First Poem

My name is Kimberley and I go to preschool,
My best friend is Lily, who is really cool.
I watch Charlie and Lola on TV,
Playing dressing up is lots of fun for me.
I just love cucumbers to eat,
And sometimes a Kinder egg for a treat.
Blue is a colour I like a lot,
My bike is the best present I ever got.
My favourite person is Arrib, who is a gem,
So this, my first poem, is just for them!

Kimberley Meaden (3)
Pinhoe Preschool, Exeter

My First Poem

My name is Max and I go to preschool,

My best friend is Lucas, who is really cool.

I watch Peppa Pig on TV,

Playing with dinosaurs is lots of fun for me.

I just love sausages to eat,

And sometimes a chocolate hippo for a treat.

Red is a colour I like a lot,

My tool kit is the best present I ever got.

My favourite person is Unky Sam, who is a gem,

So this, my first poem, is just for them!

Max Bowles (2)
Pinhoe Preschool, Exeter

My First Poem

My name is Louis and I go to preschool,

My best friend is Sophia, who is really cool.

I watch Team Umizoomi on TV,

Playing with trains is lots of fun for me.

I just love pasta to eat,

And sometimes chocolate cake for a treat.

Green is a colour I like a lot,

My car is the best present I ever got.

My favourite person is Evan, who is a gem,

So this, my first poem, is just for them!

Louis George Le Puill (3)
Pinhoe Preschool, Exeter

My First Poem

My name is Isabella and I go to preschool,

My best friend is Ruby, who is really cool.

I watch Go Diego Go! on TV,

Playing with Mummy's Sindy dolls is lots of fun

for me.

I just love ice cream and pop-pops to eat,

And sometimes a chocolate egg for a treat.

Purple is a colour I like a lot,

My cuddly Chase doggy is the best present I ever

got.

My favourite person is my mummy, who is a gem,

So this, my first poem, is just for them!

Isabella Rose Perks (3)

Pinhoe Preschool, Exeter

My First Poem

My name is Megan and I go to preschool,

My best friend is Lottie, who is really cool.

I watch Frozen on TV,

Playing with Jack is lots of fun for me.

I just love pasta to eat,

And sometimes chocolate for a treat.

Pink is a colour I like a lot,

My Anna is the best present I ever got.

My favourite person is my brother, Jack, who is a

gem,

So this, my first poem, is just for him!

Megan Hubbleday (3)

Pinhoe Preschool, Exeter

177

My First Poem

My name is Lois and I go to preschool,

My best friend is Emily, who is really cool.

I watch Peppa Pig on TV,

Playing with baby dolls is lots of fun for me.

I just love sandwiches to eat,

And sometimes pink ice cream for a treat.

Pink is a colour I like a lot,

My baby, Emily, is the best present I ever got.

My favourite person is Mummy, who is a gem,

So this, my first poem, is just for them!

Lois Chan (3)
Pinhoe Preschool, Exeter

My First Poem

My name is Janelle and I go to preschool,

My best friend is Zoe, who is really cool.

I watch Peppa Pig on TV,

Playing with my toys is lots of fun for me.

I just love spaghetti to eat,

And sometimes chocolate for a treat.

Pink is a colour I like a lot,

My doll house is the best present I ever got.

My favourite person is Olivier, who is a gem,

So this, my first poem, is just for them!

Janelle Lola Nwabuzor (4)
Pinhoe Preschool, Exeter

My First Poem

My name is Ashia and I go to preschool,

My best friend is my mummy, who is really cool.

I watch Scooby-Doo, Peppa Pig and Toot Toot

the Tiny Tug Boat on TV,

Playing with Lucy, Zara, Isabella and Lexi is lots

of fun for me.

I just love spaghetti Bolognese to eat,

And sometimes ice cream for a treat.

Pink is a colour I like a lot,

My kitchen is the best present I ever got.

My favourite person is my daddy, who is a gem,

So this, my first poem, is just for them!

Ashia Lambert (4)

Pinhoe Preschool, Exeter

My First Poem

My name is Charlie and I go to preschool,

My best friend is Regan, who is really cool.

I watch PAW Patrol on TV,

Playing hide-and-seek is lots of fun for me.

I just love Pringles to eat,

And sometimes sweeties for a treat.

Orange is a colour I like a lot,

My Imaginext police robot is the best present I

ever got.

My favourite person is Daddy, who is a gem,

So this, my first poem, is just for them!

Charlie Goode (4)
Pinhoe Preschool, Exeter

My First Poem

My name is Zara and I go to preschool,

My best friend is Ashia, who is really cool.

I watch PAW Patrol on TV,

Playing shopping with my trolley is lots of fun for

me.

I just love pain au chocolat to eat,

And sometimes sweeties and chocolate for a

treat.

Purple is a colour I like a lot,

My Christmas scooter is the best present I ever

got.

My favourite person is Alisa, who is a gem,

So this, my first poem, is just for them!

Zara Imogen Adlem (3)
Pinhoe Preschool, Exeter

My First Poem

My name is Bobby-Lee and I go to preschool,

My best friend is Oo-Oo the monkey, who is really cool.

I watch Scooby-Doo on TV,

Playing with the Play-Doh at Nanny's is lots of fun for me.

I just love cheese, grapes, bananas and toast to eat,

And sometimes a Kinder egg for a treat.

Orange is a colour I like a lot,

My dinosaur is the best present I ever got.

My favourite person is Nanny, who is a gem,

So this, my first poem, is just for them!

Bobby-Lee Gliddon (3)
Pinhoe Preschool, Exeter

My First Poem

My name is Holly and I go to preschool,

My best friend is Lizzy, who is really cool.

I watch Bing and Peppa Pig on TV,

Playing with sand and animals is lots of fun for

me.

I just love Marmite on toast to eat,

And sometimes chocolate ice cream with a

Flake and sprinkles for a treat.

Pink is a colour I like a lot,

My fish, Goldie is the best present I ever got.

My favourite person is Daddy, who is a gem,

So this, my first poem, is just for them!

Holly Ella Stevens (3)
Pinhoe Preschool, Exeter

My First Poem

My name is Tyler and I go to preschool,

My best friend is Irem, who is really cool.

I watch chickens on TV,

Playing Batman games is lots of fun for me.

I just love red apples to eat,

And sometimes Kinder eggs and sweets for a

treat.

Red is a colour I like a lot,

My Superman is the best present I ever got.

My favourite person is Mummy, who is a gem,

So this, my first poem, is just for them!

Tyler Simpson (3)
Pip-Kins Day Nursery, Exeter

My First Poem

My name is Rylan and I go to preschool,

My best friend is my Dan, who is really cool.

I watch Cars, the movie, on TV,

Playing with lots of cars is lots of fun for me.

I just love egg on toast to eat,

And sometimes ice cream for a treat.

Blue is a colour I like a lot,

My big bouncy ball is the best present I ever got.

My favourite person is Mummy, who is a gem,

So this, my first poem, is just for them!

Rylan Nicholas Baker (3)
Pip-Kins Day Nursery, Exeter

My First Poem

My name is Olivia and I go to preschool,

My best friend is Charlotte, who is really cool.

I watch Peppa Pig on TV,

Playing with my toys with Mummy is lots of fun

for me.

I just love pasta to eat,

And sometimes sweeties for a treat.

Yellow is a colour I like a lot,

My daddy's slippers are the best present I ever got.

My favourite person is Mummy, who is a gem,

So this, my first poem, is just for them!

Olivia Taylor (3)
Pip-Kins Day Nursery, Exeter

My First Poem

My name is Florence and I go to preschool,

My best friend is my sister, who is really cool.

I watch Aladdin on TV,

Playing with my mummy is lots of fun for me.

I just love sausage rolls to eat,

And sometimes grapes for a treat.

Pink is a colour I like a lot,

My baby is the best present I ever got.

My favourite person is Mummy, who is a gem,

So this, my first poem, is just for them!

Florence Hall (2)
Pip-Kins Day Nursery, Exeter

My First Poem

My name is Saphy Angel and I go to preschool,

My best friend is Samuel, who is really cool.

I watch Peppa Pig on TV,

Playing house games is lots of fun for me.

I just love choc choc to eat,

And sometimes grapes for a treat.

Blue is a colour I like a lot,

My baby doll is the best present I ever got.

My favourite person is Mummy, who is a gem,

So this, my first poem, is just for them!

Saphyre Chinyere Igwe (2)
Pip-Kins Day Nursery, Exeter

My First Poem

My name is Lara and I go to preschool,

My best friend is Aylie, who is really cool.

I watch CBeebies on TV,

Playing with the doctors set is lots of fun for me.

I just love bacon and salmon to eat,

And sometimes sweeties for a treat.

Pink is a colour I like a lot,

My Doc Mobile is the best present I ever got.

My favourite person is Olivia, who is a gem,

So this, my first poem, is just for them!

Lara Owen (3)
Pip-Kins Day Nursery, Exeter

My First Poem

My name is Mila and I go to preschool,

My best friend is Cat, who is really cool.

I watch Peppa on TV,

Playing with toys is lots of fun for me.

I just love pasta to eat,

And sometimes chocolate cake for a treat.

Pink is a colour I like a lot,

My Peppa Pink toy is the best present I ever got.

My favourite person is Cat, who is a gem,

So this, my first poem, is just for them!

Mila Rose Daniel (2)
Roger's Burrow Nursery, Plymouth

191

My First Poem

My name is Amy and I go to preschool,

My best friend is Eilidh, who is really cool.

I watch Peppa Pig on TV,

Playing with Eilidh is lots of fun for me.

I just love healthy food to eat,

And sometimes chocolate for a treat.

Pink is a colour I like a lot,

My bike is the best present I ever got.

My favourite person is Mummy, who is a gem,

So this, my first poem, is just for them!

Amy Edmonds (3)

Roger's Burrow Nursery, Plymouth

My First Poem

My name is Maddison and I go to preschool,

My best friend is Mummy, who is really cool.

I watch Peppa Pig on TV,

Playing mums and dads is lots of fun for me.

I just love a snack to eat,

And sometimes sweeties for a treat.

Red is a colour I like a lot,

My dolly is the best present I ever got.

My favourite person is Mummy, who is a gem,

So this, my first poem, is just for them!

Maddison Tyler (2)
Roger's Burrow Nursery, Plymouth

My First Poem

My name is Jack and I go to preschool,

My best friend is Noah, who is really cool.

I watch Flushed Away on TV,

Playing at home is lots of fun for me.

I just love pasta to eat,

And sometimes Costa coffee for a treat.

Orange is a colour I like a lot,

My Fireman Sam truck is the best present I ever

got.

My favourite person is Cat, who is a gem,

So this, my first poem, is just for them!

Jack Anthony Fendyke (3)
Roger's Burrow Nursery, Plymouth

My First Poem

My name is Arthur and I go to preschool,

My best friend is Mummy, who is really cool.

I watch racing cars on TV,

Playing with monster trucks is lots of fun for me.

I just love yoghurt to eat,

And sometimes biscuits for a treat.

Blue is a colour I like a lot,

My Monster Truck is the best present I ever got.

My favourite person is Mummy, who is a gem,

So this, my first poem, is just for them!

Arthur Netherton-Hind (3)
St Teath Preschool, Bodmin

My First Poem

My name is Jack and I go to preschool,

My best friend is Ben, my brother, who is really cool.

I watch Star Wars on TV,

Playing dinosaur games is lots of fun for me.

I just love pasties to eat,

And sometimes chocolate for a treat.

Blue is a colour I like a lot,

My Star Wars Lego is the best present I ever got.

My favourite person is Mummy, who is a gem,

So this, my first poem, is just for them!

Jack Grey (4)
St Teath Preschool, Bodmin

My First Poem

My name is Ryan and I go to preschool,

My best friend is Aaron, my brother, who is really cool.

I watch Fireman Sam on TV,

Playing with cars is lots of fun for me.

I just love rice to eat,

And sometimes chocolate for a treat.

White is a colour I like a lot,

My Fireman Sam is the best present I ever got.

My favourite person is Aaron, I love him, who is a gem,

So this, my first poem, is just for them!

Ryan Wren (3)
St Teath Preschool, Bodmin

My First Poem

My name is Poppy and I go to preschool,

My best friend is Lils, who is really cool.

I watch Sofia the First on TV,

Playing princesses is lots of fun for me.

I just love chips to eat,

And sometimes a Kinder egg for a treat.

Pink is a colour I like a lot,

My Ariel princess is the best present I ever got.

My favourite person is Izzy, who is a gem,

So this, my first poem, is just for them!

Poppy Hawkey (4)
St Teath Preschool, Bodmin

My First Poem

My name is Jasmine and I go to preschool,

My best friend is Ruby, who is really cool.

I watch Doc McStuffins on TV,

Playing babies, mummies and daddies is lots of

fun for me.

I just love spaghetti Bolognese to eat,

And sometimes cake for a treat.

Red is a colour I like a lot,

My Doc McStuffins is the best present I ever got.

My favourite person is Lara, who is a gem,

So this, my first poem, is just for them!

Jasmine McMillan (4)
St Teath Preschool, Bodmin

My First Poem

My name is Keira and I go to preschool,

My best friend is Jasmine, who is really cool.

I watch Peppa Pig on TV,

Playing mummy and babies is lots of fun for me.

I just love fish and chips to eat,

And sometimes chocolate for a treat.

Pink is a colour I like a lot,

My buggy is the best present I ever got.

My favourite person is Alfie, who is a gem,

So this, my first poem, is just for them!

Keira Emily Florry Burnard (4)

St Teath Preschool, Bodmin

My First Poem

My name is Mason and I go to preschool,

My best friend is Jack, who is really cool.

I watch Cars on TV,

Playing Hulk Smash! is lots of fun for me.

I just love a fruit pot to eat,

And sometimes surprise eggs for a treat.

Blue is a colour I like a lot,

My big Hulk is the best present I ever got.

My favourite person is Hulk, who is a gem,

So this, my first poem, is just for them!

Mason Mountain (2)
St Teath Preschool, Bodmin

My First Poem

My name is Logan and I go to preschool,

My best friend is Lara, who is really cool.

I watch Transformers on TV,

Playing car games is lots of fun for me.

I just love carrot sticks and humous to eat,

And sometimes chocolate for a treat.

Green is a colour I like a lot,

My quad bike is the best present I ever got.

My favourite person is Codey, who is a gem,

So this, my first poem, is just for them!

Logan Masters (3)
St Teath Preschool, Bodmin

202

My First Poem

My name is Lara and I go to preschool,

My best friend is Ryan, who is really cool.

I watch Peter Rabbit on TV,

Playing princesses is lots of fun for me.

I just love brioche rolls to eat,

And sometimes sweeties for a treat.

Blue is a colour I like a lot,

My Playmobil is the best present I ever got.

My favourite person is Rowan, who is a gem,

So this, my first poem, is just for them!

Lara Turner (4)
St Teath Preschool, Bodmin

 My First Poem

My name is Tom and I go to preschool,

My best friend is Enzo, who is really cool.

I watch Teenage Mutant Ninja Turtles on TV,

Playing dinosaur games is lots of fun for me.

I just love pizza to eat,

And sometimes sweeties for a treat.

Blue is a colour I like a lot,

My motorbike is the best present I ever got.

My favourite person is cousin, Jack, who is a gem,

So this, my first poem, is just for them!

Tom Harris (4)
St Teath Preschool, Bodmin

My First Poem

My name is Ryley and I go to preschool,

My best friend is my Logan, who is really cool.

I watch Postman Pat on TV,

Playing with friends is lots of fun for me.

I just love humous and pitta bread to eat,

And sometimes sweeties for a treat.

Red is a colour I like a lot,

My Dyson Hoover is the best present I ever got.

My favourite person is Mummy, who is a gem,

So this, my first poem, is just for them!

Ryley Dean James Mountain (3)
St Teath Preschool, Bodmin

205

My First Poem

My name is Millie and I go to preschool,

My best friend is Daddy, who is really cool.

I watch Minnie Mouse on TV,

Playing Minnie Mouse Boutique games is lots of

fun for me.

I just love brioche rolls to eat,

And sometimes a Kinder egg for a treat.

Pink is a colour I like a lot,

My pair of glittery socks is the best present I ever

got.

My favourite person is Mummy, who is a gem,

So this, my first poem, is just for them!

Millie Wood (3)
St Teath Preschool, Bodmin

My First Poem

My name is Bailey and I go to preschool,

My best friend is Enzo, who is really cool.

I watch Melody on TV,

Playing with flowers is lots of fun for me.

I just love sausages to eat,

And sometimes sweeties for a treat.

Red is a colour I like a lot,

My ballerina is the best present I ever got.

My favourite person is Mummy, who is a gem,

So this, my first poem, is just for them!

Bailey McIlroy (3)
St Teath Preschool, Bodmin

My First Poem

My name is Logan and I go to preschool,

My best friend is Lara, who is really cool.

I watch Ninja Turtles on TV,

Playing Avengers games is lots of fun for me.

I just love jacket potato to eat,

And sometimes sweeties for a treat.

Red is a colour I like a lot,

My Lego is the best present I ever got.

My favourite person is Uncle Matt, who is a gem,

So this, my first poem, is just for them!

Logan Nicholas Mark Mountain (4)
St Teath Preschool, Bodmin

My First Poem

My name is Enzo and I go to preschool,

My best friend is Tom, who is really cool.

I watch Transformers on TV,

Playing Big Hero 6 games is lots of fun for me.

I just love sausages and pasta to eat,

And sometimes sweeties for a treat.

Blue is a colour I like a lot,

My digger with a scoop on the front is the best

present I ever got.

My favourite person is Daddy, who is a gem,

So this, my first poem, is just for them!

Enzo John Davoust-Zangari (4)
St Teath Preschool, Bodmin

My First Poem

My name is Evie and I go to preschool,

My best friend is Mummy, who is really cool.

I watch Ben and Holly on TV,

Playing babies is lots of fun for me.

I just love sandwiches to eat,

And sometimes sweets for a treat.

Pink is a colour I like a lot,

My Frozen bowl is the best present I ever got.

My favourite person is Mollie, who is a gem,

So this, my first poem, is just for them!

Evie Maya Hope (4)
Sara' School Preschool, Exeter

210

My First Poem

My name is Bridget and I go to preschool,

My best friend is Fin, who is really cool.

I watch Frozen on TV,

Playing Hickory Dickory Dock is lots of fun for me.

I just love fish to eat,

And sometimes jelly for a treat.

Blue is a colour I like a lot,

My skipping rope is the best present I ever got.

My favourite person is Mummy, who is a gem,

So this, my first poem, is just for them!

Bridget Dunning (3)
Sara' School Preschool, Exeter

211

My First Poem

My name is Lily and I go to preschool,

My best friend is Freya, who is really cool.

I watch CBeebies on TV,

Playing Barbie games is lots of fun for me.

I just love Daddy's roast to eat,

And sometimes pick 'n' mix for a treat.

Red is a colour I like a lot,

My Furby is the best present I ever got.

My favourite person is Nannie, who is a gem,

So this, my first poem, is just for them!

Lily Welsh (3)
Sara' School Preschool, Exeter

212

My First Poem

My name is Isla and I go to preschool,

My best friend is Zara, who is really cool.

I watch Peppa Pig on TV,

Playing Bella games is lots of fun for me.

I just love fish and chips to eat,

And sometimes Quality Street for a treat.

Yellow is a colour I like a lot,

My hula hoop is the best present I ever got.

My favourite person is Zara, who is a gem,

So this, my first poem, is just for them!

Isla Jordan (3)
Sara' School Preschool, Exeter

My First Poem

My name is Mia and I go to preschool,

My best friend is Harry, who is really cool.

I watch Frozen on TV,

Playing Elsa games is lots of fun for me.

I just love Chinese food to eat,

And sometimes yoghurt for a treat.

Pink is a colour I like a lot,

My Elsa is the best present I ever got.

My favourite person is Nana, who is a gem,

So this, my first poem, is just for them!

Mia Bailey (3)
Sara' School Preschool, Exeter

My First Poem

My name is Keely and I go to preschool,

My best friend is Courtney, who is really cool.

I watch Minions on TV,

Playing with dolls is lots of fun for me.

I just love chicken nuggets to eat,

And sometimes sweets for a treat.

Orange is a colour I like a lot,

My pink baby is the best present I ever got.

My favourite person is Mummy, who is a gem,

So this, my first poem, is just for them!

Keely Lowton (3)
Sara' School Preschool, Exeter

My First Poem

My name is Mollie and I go to preschool,

My best friend is Evie, who is really cool.

I watch Peppa Pig on TV,

Playing babies is lots of fun for me.

I just love chicken nuggets to eat,

And sometimes chocolate for a treat.

Pink is a colour I like a lot,

My Frozen bowl is the best present I ever got.

My favourite person is Mummy, who is a gem,

So this, my first poem, is just for them!

Mollie Hope (2)
Sara' School Preschool, Exeter

My First Poem

My name is William and I go to preschool,

My best friend is Daddy, who is really cool.

I watch Tractor Ted on TV,

Playing tractor games is lots of fun for me.

I just love apples to eat,

And sometimes sweets for a treat.

Blue is a colour I like a lot,

My tractor is the best present I ever got.

My favourite person is Mummy, who is a gem,

So this, my first poem, is just for them!

William Taylor (2)
Sara' School Preschool, Exeter

My First Poem

My name is Taylor and I go to preschool,

My best friend is Daddy, who is really cool.

I watch Topsy and Tim on TV,

Playing car games is lots of fun for me.

I just love pasta to eat,

And sometimes biscuits for a treat.

Purple is a colour I like a lot,

My Peter Rabbit is the best present I ever got.

My favourite person is Mummy, who is a gem,

So this, my first poem, is just for them!

Taylor Smaldon (2)

Sara' School Preschool, Exeter

218

My First Poem

My name is Ciaran and I go to preschool,

My best friend is Rokko, who is really cool.

I watch Ben 10 on TV,

Playing Power Rangers games is lots of fun for me.

I just love winner winner chicken dinner to eat,

And sometimes chocolate eggs for a treat.

Red is a colour I like a lot,

My quad bike is the best present I ever got.

My favourite person is Ryan, who is a gem,

So this, my first poem, is just for them!

Ciaran Barton (4)
Starcross Playgroup, Exeter

My First Poem

My name is Aiden and I go to preschool,

My best friend is Rokko, who is really cool.

I watch Power Rangers on TV,

Playing Power Rangers is lots of fun for me.

I just love winner winner chicken dinner to eat,

And sometimes chocolate eggs for a treat.

Blue is a colour I like a lot,

My quad bike is the best present I ever got.

My favourite person is Ryan, who is a gem,

So this, my first poem, is just for them!

Aiden Barton (4)
Starcross Playgroup, Exeter

My First Poem

My name is Thomas and I go to preschool,

My best friend is Blake, who is really cool.

I watch Umizoomi on TV,

Playing catch is lots of fun for me.

I just love pasta to eat,

And sometimes chocolate for a treat.

Blue is a colour I like a lot,

My dinosaur is the best present I ever got.

My favourite person is Jenna, my sister, who is a

gem,

So this, my first poem, is just for them!

Thomas Soldi (3)
Starcross Playgroup, Exeter

My First Poem

My name is Jayden and I go to preschool,

My best friend is Joseph, who is really cool.

I watch Tree Fu Tom on TV,

Playing dressing up and play fighting is lots of
fun for me.

I just love cucumber, sausages and chips to eat,

And sometimes chocolate and ice cream for a
treat.

Blue is a colour I like a lot,

My Ninja Turtle action figure is the best present I
ever got.

My favourite person is Jack, who is a gem,

So this, my first poem, is just for them!

Jayden Campbell (3)
Starcross Playgroup, Exeter

My First Poem

My name is Elsie and I go to preschool,

My best friend is Rose, who is really cool.

I watch Topsy and Tim and Curious George on TV,

Playing babies is lots of fun for me.

I just love lollipops to eat,

And sometimes ice cream for a treat.

Pink is a colour I like a lot,

My bike is the best present I ever got.

My favourite person is Mummy, who is a gem,

So this, my first poem, is just for them!

Elsie Rose Pearson (4)
Starcross Playgroup, Exeter

223

My First Poem

My name is Connie and I go to preschool,

My best friend is Rose, who is really cool.

I watch Sofia the First on TV,

Playing with Alfie is lots of fun for me.

I just love chocolate to eat,

And sometimes ice pops for a treat.

Pink is a colour I like a lot,

My Sofia dress is the best present I ever got.

My favourite person is Rose, who is a gem,

So this, my first poem, is just for them!

Connie Drew McLellan (4)
Starcross Playgroup, Exeter

My First Poem

My name is Rose and I go to preschool,

My best friend is Elsie, who is really cool.

I watch Frozen on TV,

Playing with Connie is lots of fun for me.

I just love fruit to eat,

And sometimes chocolate for a treat.

Purple is a colour I like a lot,

My Elsa dress is the best present I ever got.

My favourite people are my boys (twin brothers),

who are gems,

So this, my first poem, is just for them!

Rose Chloe Williams (4)
Starcross Playgroup, Exeter

225

My First Poem

My name is Archie and I go to preschool,

My best friend is Cameron, who is really cool.

I watch dinosaurs on TV,

Playing with cars is lots of fun for me.

I just love fruit to eat,

And sometimes chocolate for a treat.

Red is a colour I like a lot,

My big dinosaur is the best present I ever got.

My favourite person is Charlie, who is a gem,

So this, my first poem, is just for them!

Archie David Hudd (4)
Starcross Playgroup, Exeter

My First Poem

My name is Lily-May and I go to preschool,

My best friend is Taya, who is really cool.

I watch Ben and Holly on TV,

Playing with puzzles is lots of fun for me.

I just love chicken to eat,

And sometimes ice lollies for a treat.

Pink is a colour I like a lot,

My baby doll is the best present I ever got.

My favourite person is Daddy, who is a gem,

So this, my first poem, is just for them!

Lilly-May White (3)
Starcross Playgroup, Exeter

227

My First Poem

My name is Sian and I go to preschool,

My best friend is Isabella, who is really cool.

I watch Mickey Mouse on TV,

Playing with Build-A-Bear is lots of fun for me.

I just love grapes to eat,

And sometimes chocolate for a treat.

Pink is a colour I like a lot,

My bike is the best present I ever got.

My favourite person is Mummy, who is a gem,

So this, my first poem, is just for them!

Sian Foster (4)
Starcross Playgroup, Exeter

My First Poem

My name is Jessica and I go to preschool,

My best friend is Chloe, who is really cool.

I watch Frozen on TV,

Playing mums and dads is lots of fun for me.

I just love jam on lollipops to eat,

And sometimes crispies for a treat.

Pink is a colour I like a lot,

My pram is the best present I ever got.

My favourite person is Jordan, who is a gem,

So this, my first poem, is just for them!

Jessica Mahy (4)
Starcross Playgroup, Exeter

My First Poem

My name is Rokko and I go to preschool,

My best friend is Aiden, who is really cool.

I watch Power Rangers on TV,

Playing car games is lots of fun for me.

I just love ham sandwiches to eat,

And sometimes chocolate for a treat.

Blue is a colour I like a lot,

My motocross bike is the best present I ever got.

My favourite person is Daddy, who is a gem,

So this, my first poem, is just for them!

Rokko Redman (3)

Starcross Playgroup, Exeter

My First Poem

My name is Brooke and I go to preschool,

My best friend is Sienna, who is really cool.

I watch Ben and Holly on TV,

Playing with dollies and the doll's house is lots

of fun for me.

I just love beans on toast to eat,

And sometimes chocolate eggs for a treat.

Pink is a colour I like a lot,

My Anna dolly is the best present I ever got.

My favourite person is Katie-Jayne, who is a gem,

So this, my first poem, is just for them!

Brooke Heyda (4)
Sticklebricks Preschool, Barnstaple

My First Poem

My name is Daniel and I go to preschool,

My best friend is Matthew, who is really cool.

I watch Minions on TV,

Playing ice ninjas is lots of fun for me.

I just love beans on toast to eat,

And sometimes yoghurts for a treat.

Red is a colour I like a lot,

My Ice Ninja is the best present I ever got.

My favourite person is Luke, who is a gem,

So this, my first poem, is just for them!

Daniel Higgs (4)
Sticklebricks Preschool, Barnstaple

My First Poem

My name is Luke and I go to preschool,

My best friend is Daniel, who is really cool.

I watch Ninjas on TV,

Playing hide-and-seek is lots of fun for me.

I just love sandwiches to eat,

And sometimes a yoghurt for a treat.

Red is a colour I like a lot,

My Buzz Lightyear walkie talkie is the best

present I ever got.

My favourite person is Matthew, who is a gem,

So this, my first poem, is just for them!

Luke Higgs (4)
Sticklebricks Preschool, Barnstaple

233

My First Poem

My name is Amelia and I go to preschool,

My best friend is Chloe, who is really cool.

I watch Peppa Pig on TV,

Playing with train tracks is lots of fun for me.

I just love cookies to eat,

And sometimes apples for a treat.

Pink is a colour I like a lot,

My puzzles are the best present I ever got.

My favourite person is Maya, who is a gem,

So this, my first poem, is just for them!

Amelia Wyszomirska (4)

Sticklebricks Preschool, Barnstaple

My First Poem

My name is Maya and I go to preschool,

My best friend is Lana, who is really cool.

I watch Sofia on TV,

Playing on the slide is lots of fun for me.

I just love sandwiches to eat,

And sometimes a yoghurt for a treat.

Purple is a colour I like a lot,

My cuddle ball is the best present I ever got.

My favourite person is Kai, who is a gem,

So this, my first poem, is just for them!

Maya Duhig (3)
Sticklebricks Preschool, Barnstaple

My First Poem

My name is Lana and I go to preschool,

My best friend is Maya, who is really cool.

I watch Frozen on TV,

Playing with my Peppa Pig toys is lots of fun for

me.

I just love crisps to eat,

And sometimes chocolate for a treat.

Purple is a colour I like a lot,

My little blanket is the best present I ever got.

My favourite person is my big brother, Sebastian,

who is a gem,

So this, my first poem, is just for them!

Lana Toms (3)
Sticklebricks Preschool, Barnstaple

My First Poem

My name is Finlee and I go to preschool,

My best friend is Luke, who is really cool.

I watch Fireman Sam and Power Rangers on TV,

Playing Iron Man games is lots of fun for me.

I just love chips and sauce to eat,

And sometimes chocolate for a treat.

Red is a colour I like a lot,

My blue robot is the best present I ever got.

My favourite person is Sebastian, who is a gem,

So this, my first poem, is just for them!

Finlee Biggs (4)
Sticklebricks Preschool, Barnstaple

237

My First Poem

My name is Sebastian and I go to preschool,
My best friend is Brooke, who is really cool.
I watch Scooby-Doo on TV,
Playing chicken and egg is lots of fun for me.
I just love cheese to eat,
And sometimes chocolate for a treat.
Blue is a colour I like a lot,
My silver car is the best present I ever got.
My favourite person is Mummy , who is a gem,
So this, my first poem, is just for them!

Sebastian David Toms (4)
Sticklebricks Preschool, Barnstaple

My First Poem

My name is Sienna and I go to preschool,

My best friend is Brooke, who is really cool.

I watch Peppa Pig on TV,

Playing on the bike is lots of fun for me.

I just love potatoes and sausages to eat,

And sometimes a Kinder egg for a treat.

Pink is a colour I like a lot,

My Elsa doll is the best present I ever got.

My favourite person is my brother Alfie, who is a

gem,

So this, my first poem, is just for them!

Sienna Rose Miller (3)
Sticklebricks Preschool, Barnstaple

239

My First Poem

My name is Chloe and I go to preschool,

My best friend is Sienna, who is really cool.

I watch Peppa Pig on TV,

Playing with the kitchen is lots of fun for me.

I just love crackers and vegetables to eat,

And sometimes chocolate eggs for a treat.

Pink is a colour I like a lot,

My Elsa dolly is the best present I ever got.

My favourite person is Sienna, who is a gem,

So this, my first poem, is just for them!

Chloe Bella Savage (3)
Sticklebricks Preschool, Barnstaple

My First Poem

We hope you have enjoyed reading this book – and that you will continue to enjoy it in the coming years.

If you're a young writer who enjoys reading and creative writing, or the parent of an enthusiastic poet or story writer, do visit our websites, www.myfirstpoem.com and www.youngwriters.co.uk. Here you will find free competitions, workshops and games, as well as recommended reads, a poetry glossary and our blog.

If you would like to order further copies of this book, or any of our other titles, then please give us a call or visit www.myfirstpoem.com.

My First Poem
Remus House
Coltsfoot Drive
Peterborough
PE2 9BF

Tel: 01733 898110
info@myfirstpoem.com